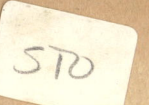

Slavic Civilization
Through The Ages

LONDON : GEOFFREY CUMBERLEGE
OXFORD UNIVERSITY PRESS

Slavic Civilization

Through The Ages

BY
SAMUEL HAZZARD CROSS
EDITED WITH A FOREWORD BY
Leonid I. Strakhovsky

HARVARD UNIVERSITY PRESS
CAMBRIDGE, MASSACHUSETTS
1948

COPYRIGHT, 1948
BY THE PRESIDENT AND FELLOWS OF HARVARD COLLEGE

PRINTED BY THE COLONIAL PRESS INC.
CLINTON, MASSACHUSETTS, U. S. A.

FOREWORD

The late Dr. Samuel Hazzard Cross, Professor of Slavic Languages and Literatures at Harvard University, left a complete manuscript of the eight lectures he delivered at the Lowell Institute of Boston in November and December of 1939. It became my pleasant duty to edit them for publication, but in doing so I have revised only the form of the lectures and not their content.

Fortified by years of research and teaching in the field, Professor Cross paints in a broad sweep the picture of the rise, fall, and reëmergence of the three branches of the Slavic people—the Eastern, the Western, and the Southern. He describes the origins of many of the sources of modern conflicts such as the struggles between German and Pole, and Pole and Russian; the quest of Poland to obtain lands to the Elbe river which Poles had once occupied; the desire of Russia to dominate the eastern shores of the Baltic Sea; the conflict between German and Czech over the Sudeten area; the lack of cohesion and statesmanship among the Southern Slavs. Mr. Cross also evaluates the great cultural contribution of the Germans to their Slavic neighbors which the latter have often minimized for political and nationalistic reasons. He assails the romantic notion of the "mission" supposedly inherent in any nation or racial group and points out that the real contribution of the Slavic people to world civilization is the result of achievement recognizable as such by other people and not the result of so-called "missionary" activity. While analyzing the origins of modern conflicts, Mr. Cross gives a profound evaluation not only of the basic similarity of Slavic cultures, but also of the reasons for their dissimilarity produced on the whole by geographical conditions as well as by foreign influences.

For all those who want to understand what has been happening in recent times in eastern and central Europe Mr. Cross has provided an indispensable historical survey. The reader will find himself drawn rapidly on through an informative and fascinating study of Slavic civilization, written by a scholar, a teacher, and a brilliant lecturer whose untimely passing left a chasm in the field of Slavic studies.

Leonid I. Strakhovsky

Contents

I	*The Primitive Slavs*	1
II	*The Slavic Migrations*	27
III	*Conversion and Religious Divisions*	52
IV	*The Formation of Russia*	75
V	*Foundations of Russian Culture*	98
VI	*German and Slav*	121
VII	*The Balkan Principalities*	143
VIII	*Servitude and Liberation*	164
IX	*Conclusion*	177

Slavic Civilization
Through The Ages

I

The Primitive Slavs

The object of this study is to provide a fairly detailed account of the Slavs from their first appearance in history to their emergence in modern times as a group of nations akin in race and language, but diversified by the cultural and political influences to which they have been exposed.

Numerically the Slavs are the largest linguistic group in Europe, including some two hundred million people. Located in the eastern section of the European Continent, they were long remote from the civilization which grew up on the northern shore of the Mediterranean, and thus were late in assuming an active political role. In early medieval times their lack of organization made them an easy prey to nations of higher material culture and more intense political aspirations; consequently the hostility between German and Slav is a historical factor of long standing. The geographical situation of the Slavs not only set them as a natural bulwark against nomadic invaders from Asia, but also exposed them to Asiatic cultural influences and to the infusion of alien blood. Their very numbers and their remote habitations retarded their cultural advance, as did also the domination of the unenlightened mass by an intelligent minority touched in varying degree by foreign civilizations. Hence the absence of any pervasive tradition of native culture has repeatedly prevented the development of ethnic or national self-consciousness and restricted the capacity of Slavic peoples either for self-government or for a resolute national effort in the critical moments of their evolution. Even those Slavs who live closest to the centers of European civilization and who shared its progress for centuries have often been debarred by economic and political factors from the enjoyment of a full national life, and those more distant from these centers have emerged from the Middle Ages only during the last 250 years. In the light of these facts, it is not surprising that the Slavs have often seemed an enigma to the Western world.

By virtue of their geographical distribution, the modern Slavs fall naturally into three distinct groups: Eastern, Western, and Southern. Of these, the Eastern is the most numerous. It embraces the Russians, who comprise two-thirds of the Slavic complex, and subdivide linguistically into three sections: first and most important, the so-called Great Russians, inhabiting the central and northern districts of European Russia; second, the White Russians (and here "White" has no political connotation whatever, but means light-haired) who occupy the area which borders on the northern part of the former eastern frontier of Poland, and, while centering in the neighborhood of Minsk, also run over into former Polish territory as far as Grodno, Bialystok, and Brest-Litovsk; and third, the so-called Little Russians (otherwise known as Ukrainians or Ruthenians), who inhabit the black-earth prairies or steppes north of the Black Sea from the western frontier to the Kuban and Don rivers. The Ukrainians, as present-day newspaper readers know only too well, also inhabit not only Volhynia and Eastern Galicia as far west as Przemysl, but also the extreme eastern tip of the former republic of Czechoslovakia, known as Subcarpathian Russia (now Soviet territory), and likewise make up a considerable part of the population of Bukovina (now also Soviet), an area which formerly belonged to Romania and which lies just south of the former Polish-Romanian frontier.

The Primitive Slavs 3

It was to this district, centering about the city of Czernowitz, that many Polish officials and soldiers withdrew to escape German and Russian pursuit when Poland was invaded in 1939.

The Western Slavic group includes the Poles, the Czechs (or Bohemians) and Moravians, the Slovaks, and two Slavic islands in German territory: the Kashubs, who live on the Baltic coast northwest of Danzig, probably not over two hundred thousand in number, and a considerably smaller number of Sorbs, or Wends, who inhabit Lausitz, or Lusatia, a small area on the upper Spree river northeast of Dresden.

The Southern Slavs are cut off from their northern kindred by the Austrian Germans, the Magyars, and the Romanians, but comprise the Slovenes in the extreme northern part of Yugoslavia; the Serbs and the Croatians, who differ from one another only in slight variations of dialect and by the fact that the Serbs belong to the Greek Orthodox church and use the Cyrillic Script (similar to the Russian), while the Croatians are Catholics and use the Latin alphabet; and the Bulgarians who, though possessing a Slavic national language, represent a complex fusion of racial and linguistic stocks.

In view of the numerous and violent migratory movements which took place in northern Europe both before the Christian era and during the first few centuries after it began, the Slavs are hardly likely to have occupied their present extensive territory during their whole recorded history. On the contrary, their migrations cover a range almost as vast as those of their Germanic neighbors, and the location of their primitive habitat constitutes a problem which has long engaged students of Slavic history and linguistics.

The earliest native tradition dealing with Slavic origins is contained in the so-called Russian *Primary Chronicle,* a compilation completely extant only in two fourteenth-century texts, but which reproduce with considerable accuracy a work composed by a monk of Kiev about the end of the eleventh century. Here we read:

4   *Slavic Civilization*

For many years the Slavs lived beside the Danube, where the Hungarian and the Bulgarian lands now lie. From among these Slavs parties scattered throughout the country and were known by appropriate names, according to the places where they settled. Thus some came and settled by the river Morava, and were named Moravians, while others were called Czechs. Among these same Slavs are included the White Croats, the Serbs, and the Carinthians. For when the Vlakhs attacked the Danubian Slavs, and settled among them, the latter came and made their homes by the Vistula, and were then called Lyakhs. Of these Lyakhs some were called Polyanians, some Lutichians, some Mazovians, and still others Pomorians. Certain Slavs also settled on the Dnieper, and were called Polyanians. Still others were called Derevlians, because they lived in the forests. Some also settled between the Pripet and the Dvina, and were known as Dregovichians. Other tribes settled on the Dvina and became known as Polotians, from a small stream named the Polot, which flows into the Dvina. . . . The Slavs also settled around lake Ilmen, and were there known by their own name. They built a city, and called it Novgorod. Still others had their settlements along the Desna, the Sem, and the Sula, and were called Severians. And thus the Slavic race was scattered, and likewise its language was known as Slavic.

In this passage, apart from the detail expended by the author on particularizing the various Eastern Slavic tribes which had fallen under the sway of Kiev more than two centuries before he wrote, what is most striking is his implication that neither the Western Slavs (Czechs, Moravians, and Poles) nor the Eastern Slavs were, in the annalist's view, indigenous to the areas they occupied in his day. He accepts the tradition that the original home of the Slavs was on the middle Danube, from which region (as he relates) they were displaced at an earlier undefined period by a nation known as the Vlakhs, under whose pressure they sought safer residences to the north and northeast. Now, while the term Vlakh has various meanings, it would be most natural here to attach it to the Celtic Gauls who penetrated the Danube basin early in the fourth century B.C. and then, under the leadership of a chief named Brennus, marched down through Thrace and Macedonia and invaded Greece as far as Delphi in 280. The only difficulty lies in the absence of the slightest indication in Greek or Latin historians and geographers that the Slavs, or any part of them, were present on the middle or lower Danube basin before the Christian era. Nor are there in this area any early place names demonstrably Slavic which would show these sources to be faulty in this respect.

In fact, though the evidence of this passage from the Russian annals led numerous medieval and early modern historians in the last century to accept the Danubian origin of the Slavs, other much more reliable and older sources place them further north beyond the Carpathian Mountains when they make their first appearance in history. To be sure, the Slavs do not begin their historical career under this name, but under another which is etymologically related to the English term "Wends" or the German "Wenden," frequently applied to the Slavs in our own day. As the Venedi, Veneti, or Venedae, they are thus mentioned by Pliny the Elder and by Tacitus during the first century, and by the Egyptian astronomer and geographer Claudius Ptolemy, who wrote in Greek toward the end of the second century. Pliny locates them vaguely in the vicinity of the Vistula. Tacitus is equally indefinite, placing them in the unknown country east of the Suebic confederacy, which he knew as Germanic. Ptolemy mentions them as one of the major nations living along the Venedic Gulf, which appears to be his term for the section of the Baltic coast northeast of the Vistula.

The identity of the Venedae of the Baltic with the Slavs is established in the sixth century by Jordanes, the historian of the Goths, who says of them in one passage: "From the source of the Vistula river immense areas are occupied by the populous nation of the Venethae, who, though their appellations may change in various clans and districts, are mainly called

Sclaveni and *Antae*," and adds elsewhere, "Though deriving from one stem, they have now adopted three names, that is, Venethi, Antes, and Sclaveni." The "Ravenna Cosmographer," an anonymous geographic work not later than the seventh century, mentions the *Sclavini* as living in Scythia, which is here a generic term for northeastern Europe, while the ninth-century Latin text known as the "Anonymous Bavarus," with the full title "Description of the cities and regions on the north bank of the Danube," speaks of the *Zeruiani* (the name is obviously related to the modern terms *Serb* and *Sorb*), "which is so great a realm that from it, as their tradition relates, all the tribes of the Slavs are sprung and trace their origin."

Such of these sources as belong to the sixth century or later obviously reflect a period when the Slavic dispersion had already begun, but they are interesting as early datable appearances of the name *Slav* and as a sound basis for identifying Wends and Slavs as the same people.

Linguistic evidence also impels us to place the Slavs north of the Carpathians before their dispersion. Old Slavonic not only shows traces of contacts with Thracian, Iranian, and Germanic, but is also closely related to Lithuanian and exerted some influence on the early Finnish vocabulary. The only area where such extensive relations could have developed must necessarily have been north and east of the Carpathian chain. It is likewise true that such anthropological evidence as we have identifies the proto-Slavs rather with the northern longheaded race than with the primitive Central European brachycephalics, though even at the epoch of Slavic unity the cephalic index was by no means uniform, and with the lapse of time the stronger shortheaded brunette type came to dominate among the Slavs, as it does indeed today.

The topological nomenclature of the Carpathian range is, moreover, not Slavic, thus indicating that the early Slavs lived beyond these mountains and the forests which clothed them. Furthermore, Herodotus mentions as adjacent and subject to the Scythians, but as distinct from them, a tribe known as the Neuri, who lived between the upper Dniester and the middle Dnieper rivers, and certain related Slavic place names indicate that they extended to the basins of the western Bug and the Vistula. This tribe is therefore generally regarded as Slavic, and on this basis it may be held with some certainty that the proto-Slavs as early as the fifth century B.C., and thus long before their dispersion, inhabited an area at least as far to the east as modern Kiev.

To the west it is not possible to place the proto-Slavic boundary beyond the Vistula, since all ancient historians mention this river as the eastern boundary of Germanic settlement. A further indication of this western Slavic frontier is the fact that the vocabulary of the proto-Slavs lacked a word for the beechtree, which grows west of a line roughly connecting Königsberg and Odessa, so that the Slavs were forced to borrow this name from their early Germanic neighbors. There is no good archaeological evidence to indicate that the proto-Slavs ever extended as far as the Elbe, though their medieval descendants reached it. Neither did they touch the Baltic, for the area north of the string of lakes and marshes which separates modern East Prussia from Polish territory was inhabited at the beginning of the Christian era by Baltic tribes akin to the present-day Lithuanians, who likewise occupied the basins of the Memel and the Dvina between the Slavs and the Gulf of Riga. Before the Christian era, the proto-Slavs were also separated from the Black Sea by a succession of Iranian tribes who occupied the southern steppe or prairie country, but they must have touched the navigable portions of the Russian rivers west of the Crimea, since Old Slavonic borrowed the Greek word for boat.

The habitat of the primitive Slavs before their dispersion was thus an irregular oblong area northeast of the Carpathians, extending eastward from the basin of the middle Vistula to the course of the Dnieper north and south of Kiev, bounded on the north by the rivers Narev and Pripet, and along its southern edge touching the headwaters of the Prut, the Dniester, and the Bug, which are all rivers flowing into the Black Sea.

The very origin of the names "Wend" and "Slav" is problematic. The term "Wend" has sometimes been regarded as connected with the Danish *vand,* the modern equivalent of Old Norse "vatn" (water), so that the Wends would derive this appellation from being water dwellers or lake dwellers. Though there are traces of Slavic lake dwellers, the difficulty here is that the name, being found in Pliny and Tacitus, is far older than any Slavic contacts with the Danes as such. For geographical reasons also, the earliest Slavic contacts must have been not with North Germanic, but with East Germanic tribes who (if we may judge by the Gothic vocabulary) used for water the terms "wato," without a nasal, or (in the case of a river or any body of water) "ahwa," akin to the familiar Latin "aqua." Efforts to correlate the name "Wends" with a Germanic word "wenden," to wander, so that it might signify "the wanderers," collide with the objection that both early East and West Germanic cognates of this verb simply mean "to turn," with no implication of wandering at all. Any connection with the Gothic word "winja" (pasturage) is to be rejected because of the absent dental (d), though there is abundant evidence to prove that the primitive Slavs were relatively skilful agriculturists and cattleraisers. Similarly, it is hardly possible to justify a connection between the name "Wend" and the Indo-European base *$uen,$ meaning "to strive, to wish, to love," even through such a derivative as Old Norse "vinr," friend. The Slavic etymologies proposed are even more uncertain, so that, for lack of anything better, the most reasonable supposition is that "Wend" is related to the early Celtic base "uindo," which means "white." It would thus appear that this was the appellation applied by the dark-haired Celts in the Danube basin to their blond neighbors behind the Carpathians, and this interpretation is the more appealing since there are pure Slavic tribal names of which the definition "white" or "blond" is a component, e.g., White Croats and White Russians (Belohorvaty, Belorussi).

The name "Slav" first appears in a Greek text written about 550, and from that period becomes more and more frequent. The Slavic form itself is Slověnin, plural Slověne, and corresponds, except for the inserted k and t, to the Greek and Latin Σκλαυηνοί, Στλαυηνοί, Sclaveni, Stlaveni, and it has been suggested that the shorter forms Σκλάβοι, Σθλάβοι, Sclavi, Stlavi are imitated from the numerous characteristic proper names in -slav (Vladislav, Yaroslav, Svyatoslav, etc.). The origin of the k is dubious, though it may be recalled that the initial combination sl occurs in no native Greek word, while skl, of which the sound is identical to the unpracticed ear, was familiar from οκληρός and its cognates, and stl occurs in οτλεγίς, etc. The Arabic names which include the k (Asqālab, Saqāliba) would thus appear to depend originally on these Greek forms. Among the Slavs themselves, as early as the thirteenth century, popular etymology developed a totally legendary derivation from "slava," glory, while numerous competent Slavists of the last century accepted the derivation from "slovo," word, thus interpreting *Slovene* to mean "speakers of the same language." This derivation has often been favorably argued from the converse that the Slavs called the Germans "dummies" (*nemtsy*) because their tongue was incomprehensible. On a somewhat similar basis, it has even been suggested that the name is connected with Gothic "slawan" (be silent), and English "slow," so that Slav would be a nickname like *Nemets*, as applied by the Slavs themselves to the Germans. Unfortunately, however, there is no evidence that "slawan" and "slow" are related. The trouble with both these suggestions is that the suffix *-ĕnin, -yanin* always indicates a man from a certain place, hence a *Slověnin* ought to be a man from a place called Slovo or Slava. But no such place is known. On the other hand, it has been suggested that there may have been a river or a marshy area known as Slava or Slova (the name would be akin to the Indo-European base *kleu-,* "to cleanse, to water") so that the *Slověne* would be the dwellers along the banks of such a river or in the marshy area thus postulated. In the primitive habitat of the Slavs there are rivers with names related to a base *slav-* or *slov-*, and much marshland, but nowhere has a name been preserved which is of sufficient importance to justify the assumption that it was the starting point for the term *Slověne* which, despite its mystery, has been applied to all Slavic subdivisions, whatever their location, since the sixth century A.D.

Like the Germanic dialects, the Slavic languages belong to the so-called Indo-European linguistic family. It so happens that we are familiar with a series of languages which begin to appear about 1000 B.C. from Hindustan to the Atlantic and from Scandinavia to the Mediterranean basin, and which exhibit so many common features that they may safely be considered to have a common origin. Along with the Germanic and the Slavic languages, this family includes Indo-Iranian (i.e., Sanskrit, the various later Indic dialects, and the several forms of Persian), Baltic (Lithuanian and Lettish), Albanian, Armenian, Celtic, Greek, and Italic (among the latter, besides Latin, the idioms of several other tribes speaking kindred tongues). The Baltic and the Slavic languages have so many striking resemblances that many philologists believe in a long period of Balto-Slavic community before the two branches separated and pursued individual paths of linguistic evolution. Of these two branches, the Baltic, especially as represented by Lithuanian, is the more conservative, hence evolved more slowly, and exhibits linguistically a more primitive character than Old Slavonic, despite the fact that our oldest Lithuanian text dates from the sixteenth century, while our oldest Slavic texts go back to the tenth.

While it is customary, for linguistic reasons, to postulate a uniform primitive Slavonic or proto-Slavonic tongue, this term should not be taken to mean that even at the dawn of their history the Slavic tribes over the whole extent of their habitat spoke a language identical in phonology, inflection, and vocabulary. It is rather to be supposed that the germs of dialectal differentiation inherent in the proto-Slavonic language even at the epoch of closest ethnic unity evolved into conspicuous local characteristics as the race gradually spread. By the ninth century A.D., when a Slavonic tongue was first used for literary purposes, the differentiation of the several Slavonic languages and even of the dialects in each was a consummated fact of some centuries' standing.

By their very location, remote from the centers of classical culture and bordering to the west, south, and north upon tribes to which it did not penetrate until the beginning of the Christian era, the Slavs, jutting out toward the confines of Asia in a region almost devoid of natural boundaries and barriers, were inevitably exposed to the repeated impacts of alien nations from the Orient. Destined later to form a part of the great medieval trade route from the Baltic to the Black Sea, the river Dnieper, along which the easternmost portion of the primitive Slavs lived, was likewise a promising area for penetration from the north. The Slavic occupation of western Russian territory, if the identification of Herodotus's Neuri as Slavic is correct, reaches well back toward the beginning of the first millennium before Christ. The earliest historical neighbors of the Slavs in the Russian prairie country were thus the Cimmerians, whose land, according to the *Odyssey,* was always veiled in fog and darkness, for there the sun never rose nor set. Actually they were an eastern offshoot of the Thracians, who centered in the basin west of the Carpathians until they were displaced by Germanic and Celtic invaders. During the second millennium and until the eighth century B.C., the Cimmerians extended eastward beyond the Crimea and the Sea of Azov, and to them belong the scanty remnants of bronze culture found in South Russia and dating from the beginning of the first millennium before Christ. The barrier erected by the Cimmerians to a Slavic advance toward the Black Sea was later perpetuated by the Scythians, who form the first wave of Oriental nomads to sweep across the black-earth region in historical times.

The Scythians are, in fact, the earliest inhabitants of southern Russia whose contacts with the peoples of classical antiquity permit historical definition. They were Iranians by race, hence akin to us and to the Slavs. The initial colonial outposts of the Ionian Greeks on the northern shores of the Black Sea were established in the seventh and sixth centuries B.C., and therefore almost contemporaneously with the Scythian drive against the Cimmerians. Though the latter still employed bronze implements, knowledge of the use of iron was evidently transmitted from Asia Minor about 900 B.C., and the earliest Scythian remains show South Russia to have possessed a fully developed iron-age culture.

The Scythian domination of the steppes lasted some five centuries and was of marked importance for the rise of civilization between the Volga and the Danube. The Scythians had perfected an efficient military organization which held under their sway the majority of the tribes in this region, guaranteeing them a high degree of economic prosperity by assuring the export of their produce (foodstuffs and raw materials) through the Greek trading posts of the Black Sea coastline. Embracing the whole of southern Russia, this fundamentally commercial civilization gradually extended toward the northwest. Archaeological remains between the Don and Dnieper rivers prove that prehistoric foci of population became, under the Scythians, important fortified commercial centers. Such centers appear chiefly in the district which was eventually to become the nucleus of the state dominated by Kiev, that is, in the central and eastern section of the modern Ukraine.

On the extreme west flank the Scythians extended far enough north of the Danube to collide with the troops of Alexander the Great in 325 B.C. On the east they were gradually pushed farther and farther toward the Don by the advance of a kindred Iranian tribe, the Sarmatians, who had reached that western limit by the time of Herodotus. Then, at the end of the fourth century B.C., the Sarmatians crossed the Don from their previous seats on the steppes west of the Volga, driving the Scythians before them. During the fourth and third centuries, the Scythians thus gradually transferred their nucleus from the prairie country between the Dnieper and the Don to the middle course of the Dnieper and the steppes between the Dnieper and the Bug, endeavoring to install themselves as a ruling class in the northern sections of this area and to extend their authority still further northward. This effort was vitiated by hostile contacts with other mobile ethnic units, including the Slavs.

While the Scythians had been able to set up a well-organized and centralized state in which, as their contacts with the Greek world evolved, elements of Greek civilization were grafted upon the nomadic and oriental culture which they had brought with them from Asia, they can hardly have formed at any time a majority of the population on the south Russian steppes. They were only a ruling minority, supported and enriched by the tribute in kind exacted from the subject population whose products they exported. Even the period of the fourth and third centuries B.C., during which the Scythian state was gradually declining, marked an age of great prosperity for southern Russia, since the demand for Scythian merchandise was stimulated by the influx of wealth into the Greek world after the conquests of Alexander the Great and the rise of the Hellenistic succession states.

Though racially related to the Scythians, the Sarmatians lacked their talent for organization, and first appear as a complex of disunited tribes pushed into the steppes by Mongolian movements of the fourth to the second centuries B.C. Their advance guard had penetrated as far as the Bug and the Dniester by the end of the second century. In fact, at the beginning of our era, the Sarmatians were already a menace to the Roman Empire, and their chief element, the Alans, persisted as a dominant force in South Russia till the third century A.D. Such Scythian remnants as remained in this area were absorbed by the new masters, who imitated the Scythian policy of encouraging the commerce of the Greek coastal cities whose culture they emulated. The political evolution of these Iranian residents is, however, less important than the fact that during their early history the Slavs were at least in peripheral contact with Iranian elements which had a high degree of native or acquired civilization. While their influence is reflected in a few items of the Old Slavonic vocabulary, this factor is not *per se* so significant as the continuity of cultural tradition on the southeastern border of the proto-Slavic habitat.

From their neighbors to the northeast the Slavs could derive even less intellectual stimulus. The regions east of the upper Dnieper and northward from the Dvina to the Baltic were occupied by Finnish tribes until, at the beginning of the Christian era, the Slavs, by their northeasterly advance toward the Oka and the Volga, drove a wedge between the Finnish peoples, dividing them into two sections, one of which included the Mordvinians, Cheremisses, and kindred tribes of the Volga basin west of Kazan, while the other comprised the Finnish elements which gradually approached the Baltic in the triangle between the rivers Dvina and Lovat or inhabited the region of the great lakes east of the Finnish Gulf.

It has already been mentioned that the primitive habitat of the Slavs as a whole extended as far west as the middle Vistula. As in modern times, this stream was a line of immemorial contact between Slav and German as far back as even our fragmentary historical knowledge extends. Collisions between German and Slav begin in early classical times, collisions which were usually the result of German migratory movements. The earliest on record was thus caused by the movement of the Bastarnae, who, accompanied by the Sciri, another Germanic tribe, at some epoch between the time of Herodotus (the middle of the fifth century B.C.) and 240-230 B.C., moved from their seats on the lower Vistula, hence west of the Slavs, across the western Bug (now in Polish territory) through Volhynia and Podolia, occupied by Slavs, toward the Black Sea. It is thus likely that the earliest German influences were exerted upon the Slavs by this tribe.

After the migration of the Bastarnae, the Baltic coast of eastern Germany was settled by other Germanic peoples, especially the Goths, who were present on the shoreline as early as the fourth century B.C. At any rate, in the first two Christian centuries, we find them definitely on the lower Vistula north of the Slavs. During the second century A.D. some migratory disturbance, or perhaps even the casual exploration of watercourses followed by a desire for more fertile territory and for commercial relations with the Black Sea littoral once a route thither was discovered, induced a considerable number of the Goths to move out eastward across the Bug to the basins of the Pripet and the Dniester. At some point during this movement, perhaps in Volhynia, one section split off from the main Gothic body and, after passing down the Dniester, subsequently appeared in Dacia as the Visigoths, who fought against Caracalla's troops in 214 and crossed the Danube in 248. According to the tradition preserved by Jordanes, the rest passed over the Dnieper and finally reached the coasts of the Black Sea and the Crimea.

Since the Goths remained masters of the western steppe country from the second century A.D. until 370, when they were overthrown by the Huns, they were thus the Germanic tribe with whom the proto-Slavs had the closest and most lasting relations, reflected in a considerable number of loan words in the common Slavic vocabulary. These words may be classified in groups which clearly demonstrate along what lines Gothic influence upon the Slavs was most incisive. They include an extensive list of military terms (armed band, helmet, armor, sword), commercial words (usury, debt, earring, purse, buy, kettle, plate, sack, camel, vinegar, glass), agricultural items (plow, stall, vineyard, cattle, garden, donkey, fig, bread), and names of learned professions (doctor, scribe). Some of these words point also to the probability that this borrowing either did not take place until, or at any rate was still taking place during, the period when the Germans were in close contact with the Roman Empire and had themselves already borrowed some terminology from the Latin. In any event, these words must have become ingrained in the Slavic vocabulary before 400 A.D., and made their entry into the common speech prior to the spread of the Southern Slavs into the Balkans, which began about a century later.

While for 200 years the Goths were the dominant ethnic element in southern and western Russia, they constituted only a numerically inferior ruling class which controlled the Slavic natives and such Iranian elements as were left from the period of Scythian and Sarmatian supremacy. It would otherwise be difficult to explain the process by which the Goths disappeared completely from the steppe country during the two centuries after the overthrow of the Gothic kingdom by the Huns in 370. The Huns themselves were a Turko-Tartar tribe whose western movement, begun in the first century A.D. after 300 years of strife with the Chinese in southern Mongolia, brought them to the Caspian Sea in the second. They were a nonagricultural nomadic people possessed of little culture of their own. What civilization they exhibited, and particularly their military organization, they borrowed from their Sarmatian vassals. Some of the Ostrogoths joined the advancing Huns. That portion of the Gothic population which had settled in the Crimea, though also subjected to the Huns, disappeared more slowly, and some small remnants preserved their Gothic identity as late as the eighteenth century. While the authority of the Huns does not appear to have been oppressively exercised in the steppe country, it nevertheless dealt a fatal blow to the flourishing civilization composed of combined Oriental and Greek elements which had adorned the north shore of the Black Sea for nearly a millennium. The Huns were the last Asiatic people to impinge upon the eastern section of the Slavs before their dispersion and expansion.

The primitive social organization of the early Slavs is, it must be admitted, a highly controversial subject. An exclusively patriarchal and tribal organization is found, after all, only among purely nomadic peoples, but is immediately re-

The Primitive Slavs

solved as soon as peoples become fixed, in consequence of the necessity of integrating nonkindred elements into the social complex. The originally kindred groups become contaminated with extraneous elements, though still conceived as fictitious clans or tribes. When we first encounter the Slavs, they are mostly beyond the nomadic stage, and the most primitive social unit preserved among a Slavic people in historical times is the western Serbian *Zadruga*. This characteristic family community is probably, like the Indian "joint family," a remnant not merely of Slavic but of common Indo-European antiquity.

As far as we can judge from historical survivals, the basic social unit among the early Slavs was a rural community consisting of a certain number of persons of common descent, together with outsiders who acquired membership by marriage or adoption. Its head was either its senior member or an elected chief, and direction might even devolve upon a prominent widow. The chief represented the group in external relations and directed its economy, though in serious matters he was subject to the joint decision of its membership. Collectivity of goods prevailed; the whole fortune of such a unit, together with the individual earnings of its members, belonged to the group, and could not be disposed of without common consent. Membership in such groups might run as high as over a score of households. Fields, woodland, and similar landed appendages were common property, but pasturage might be particularized. Where trade and barter became matters of vital interest (as was the case very early on the Russian watercourses), primitive towns seem to have been the creation of ambitious groups who sought a convenient point for defense or trade and then proceeded to expand their possessions and influence by the acquisition (peacefully or by violence) of adjacent interesting territory. On the other hand, patriarchal relationships might persist even in these centers. Tribal complexes such as we later encounter among the Russian Slavs derived from the union of various family units with remote ties of kinship and might attain a membership of several thousand souls. The presence of a patronymic suffix in early Russian tribal names indicates that these tribes actually passed through a stage when membership depended on kinship, but the attachment of the same suffix to place names also implies that the original implication had been forgotten before the historical period.

Prior to the evolution first of a commercial and subsequently of an official ruling class, the primitive Slavic population was divided into three distinguishable strata. At the lowest point in the scale stood the slaves, composed of captives taken in war, men who had lost their freedom for debt, and descendants of slave parents. At least in their early history, the attitude of the Slavs toward their slaves was exceedingly mild. Above the slaves stood the great group of freemen, governed by the elders of their communities and later by tribal chieftains supported by a council of elders.

Polygamy and concubinage were common to all primitive Slavs. In spite of the evidence for considerable promiscuity, a sense of the sanctity of marriage as a permanent tie is also demonstrated by early accounts of pagan Slavic wives who committed suicide upon the death of their husbands, so that the fidelity of the Slavic women was almost universally commented on with favor by foreign observers. Survivals of primitive custom among the Russian peasantry down to modern times indicate nevertheless that great freedom was allowed both sexes prior to marriage. The Slavic women enjoyed no equality in the household, though a surviving widow was authorized to take her husband's place as head of the family. Marriage by capture or by purchase was common Slavic practice.

In the course of their history, even before the dispersion, the Slavs were exposed to a series of foreign influences, especially Iranian and Germanic, which rapidly placed at their service the techniques common to adjacent ethnic groups. Linguistic evidence demonstrates that the mass of the Slavs, like the German and the Baltic peoples, was familiar with iron, gold, silver, and lead from the earliest times, at least from the second half of the first millennium B.C. The names for gold and silver are identical in all three linguistic branches, while those for iron and lead are common to both Baltic and Slavic, though differing from the German vocable. The common Slavic term for copper has no equivalent cognate in either Baltic or Germanic. Since iron became known on the coast of the Black Sea about 900 B.C., and appears in archaeological finds from the Kuban district of the northern Caucasus fully two centuries before that date, the early transmission of iron technique to the Slavs is beyond question, particularly in view of traces of iron mining and smelting in Poland even in the pre-Roman epoch. The smelting of silver and gold was, however, a post-dispersion development.

In ceramics as in metal working, the Slavs were imitators rather than pioneers. In all areas of pagan Slavic settlement we find well-turned and well-fired vases in the form of pots without handles, showing a somewhat flattened lip and ornamented, sometimes with a wavy line several times repeated, sometimes with simple horizontal stripes, and occasionally with vertical or transverse stripes or simply a series of dots in oblique lines. There is, however, nothing specifically Slavic about this technique, since it is a reproduction of the Roman vase with undulating ornament familiar in the northernmost Roman provinces between Danube and Rhine from the first to the fourth century A.D. The Slavs thus seem to have been in contact with the northern Roman markets in this interval, and gradually to have adopted the new type of pottery in preference to their own previous products of this character: high vases, or lower bowls without a flattened edge and decorated with horizontal stripes or rows of oblique lines, types developed independently of Roman influence.

Among the chief domestic industries were spinning and weaving. Since the primitive Slavs were far from expert bleachers, the resulting fabrics were mostly grayish in color. Not only is the general terminology as spinning and weaving throughout the Slavonic languages so homogeneous as to show that these techniques were a matter of common knowledge before the dispersion began, but the absence of foreign borrowings also proves it to have been a native development of very early date. It is significant that this vocabulary was taken over bodily by the Magyars upon their settlement in Central Europe.

Just as the primitive Slavs, by the moment of their dispersion, had attained a respectable technique in metal working, textiles, and ceramics (acquired in part from their neighbors), there is likewise abundant evidence that at an early stage of their existence they also possessed a knowledge of agriculture considerably in advance of what is attributed to them in this connection by frequently cited historical sources. The common Slavic vocabulary pertaining both to agriculture and to cattle-raising is in itself sufficient to vitiate any conception of the Slavs at the dawn of their history as a race of agricultural nomads leading a precarious and unstable life on scanty fare. Nor is there a sufficient number of loan-words in the Slavic vocabulary of these occupations to indicate that any appreciable proportion of the knowledge of agricultural products or livestock which the Slavs possessed was the result of contacts with other ethnic units of more advanced material culture.

The common Slavic vocabulary shows that as feed-grains the primitive Slavs knew barley, wheat, millet, rye, and oats. Among fruits they knew apples, pears, cherries, and plums. The Germans themselves knew nothing of grape culture until their migrations took them across the threshold of the Mediterranean world. Hence it is not surprising that the Slavonic words for vine and vineyard derived from the Goths, who also introduced the fig to the Slavs after Gothic settlement on the Black Sea coast. Of vegetables, the primitive Slavs consumed peas, beans, lentils, onions, garlic, and beets. Flax and hemp were familiar textile fibers. Among domestic animals, the common Slavic vocabulary includes homogeneous terms for horse, cow, bull, steer, sheep, goat, pig, and dog and, among domestic fowl, for ducks, geese, chickens, and pigeons. In these phases of culture the primitive Slavs were in no respect inferior to the primitive Germans, though the latter advanced more rapidly in proportion with their more intimate and prior contacts with the Mediterranean world. The predilection of the Slavs for agriculture is the natural consequence of their long residence in areas well suited for its practice: the plains of the Dnieper and the Vistula—though it is also likely that the epoch of the migrations and of repeated nomad incursions from Asia interrupted to some extent the sedentary tendencies and habits which the Slavs had previously developed. The primitive plow of the Slavs prior to the migrations was at first only a forked branch with one fork lopped short and cut into a point. It was later supplemented by a pole to which draft animals could be attached and a handle by which the driver could guide its course.

The primitive Slavic village varied in type. The houses might be grouped in horseshoe arrangement around a central space or in a straight line on either side of a thoroughfare. Neither of these village types appears, however, quite as primeval as the system whereby each household occupied an isolated structure in the midst of the lands its members tilled. Stone buildings were unknown. The earliest type of house consisted of a trench dug in the ground, the sides of which were raised by walls of logs stopped with earth. The wooden roof was also coated with earth as an additional protection. The primitive Slavs also erected rude log cabins without digging into the ground. We have no data on the internal furnishings of the Slavic house before the eleventh century A.D.

The chilly climate in which they lived made furs the primitive costume of the early Slavs. Furs later became an important item of Slavic export, as is shown by the early introduction of the Slavic names for squirrel and ermine into both Latin and Greek. The male costume among the early Slavs consisted of a coarse shirt falling to the knee, with sleeves and an opening for the neck, combined with wide trousers supported at the waist by a belt of rope or leather and tied in at the ankles. For the shirt they sometimes substituted a short tunic, which might be of light material or else of coarse wool, in which case it could be worn over the shirt, and it was usually buckled or pinned at the shoulder or in front of the neck. In cold weather sheepskins or the cheaper pelts (bear, wolf) were worn for warmth. Women of the people were clad in a long shirt of rough linen or hempen fabric, often representing a mere cylinder held up by straps over the shoulders. From the waist down they also wore a double apron attached to a belt, while the upper part of the body might be encased in a coarse woolen jacket, along with a cloak of similar material around the neck and shoulders. Footwear consisted of rough leather slippers held by a thong over the ankle or of slippers made of bast fiber. Men frequently wore wrapped leggings. Married women might wear a kerchief or bonnet on their heads over hair cut short, but maidens habitually went bareheaded, wearing their hair long and braided. Men also wore their hair long in the primitive period. Close shearing and shaving, where they occur, are due to foreign influences, and in general it may be said that in matters of attire the Slavs were always prompt to adopt foreign usages.

Originally a peaceful race, the primitive Slavs were unskilled in the use of weapons. When they were first noticed by foreign writers they had no offensive equipment except bows and spears, and were unprotected by even the most elementary shields. It has already been noted that in the Slavic vocabulary the words for helmet and sword were taken over from the Goths. In the succeeding centuries, the constant warfare of the migratory epoch and the necessity of defense against successive nomad incursions produced a marked amplification of Slavic military equipment representing a fusion of borrowed alien techniques so that when the southern Slavs invaded Greece at the end of the sixth century, their soldier was considered to be as good a fighter as the Byzantine regular. The Slavs, however, used no mounted troops until well into the historical period.

The Slavs were drawn very early into the orbit of European commerce, which in the peripheral areas of European antiq-

The Primitive Slavs

uity depended upon itinerant merchants and traders following strategic watercourses. Even far to the eastward, when the Goths invaded south Russian territory, they maintained the same commercial relations with the Roman Empire which had been established earlier by German settlements along its frontier further westward. Caches of Roman coins, dating chiefly from the interval between Trajan and Septimius Severus (98-198 A.D.), which have been found in great profusion on the west bank of the middle Dnieper, show a remarkable expansion of trade with the Roman west in this area during the second and third centuries, hence under the Gothic hegemony and prior to the Slavic dispersion. Once the Goths had entered into relations with Byzantium and the Greek cities on the Black Sea, their interest in trade with the western Roman Empire waned, and from that point the Dnieprian Slavs largely received products of the so-called Gothic type from the barbarized Pontic workshops. As long as the Goths lived among the Slavs, they exercised a direct economic influence upon them, but once they had withdrawn to the coast of the Black Sea after the fall of Ermanaric before the Huns in 370, they ceased to be a significant commercial factor. Even when Byzantine trade set in during the fifth century, its volume was so restricted that from this point to the eighth century there is actually an interval in which the economic relations of the Dnieper valley with the rest of the early medieval world were in abeyance.

This interval coincides with the epoch of large-scale Slavic migration and dispersion. Its conclusion is marked in turn by the stabilization of the Slavs on the Elbe, on the Danube, and in the Balkans; by the temporary elimination of nomadic invaders from the steppes, the economic advance of the Carolingian period, the beginnings of the Viking Age in Scandinavia, and the establishment of Arab control over Oriental commerce. The period from 700 to 1000, though also initiating the gradual withdrawal of the Western Slavs from the Elbe frontier under German pressure, also saw the evolution of all the medieval Slavic states and their advance to the level of contemporary material and intellectual culture which culminates in their conversion to Christianity under Roman or Byzantine auspices. It likewise witnessed an expansion of trade both in Central Europe and in the Orient, and in this commercial expansion the Slavs in general had a definite stake.

Though a combined evaluation of linguistic, source, and archaeological data permits a tolerably accurate and convincing appraisal of the material culture of the Slavs during the pagan period, there is no such coherent mass of evidence upon which any wholly satisfactory statement of their religious beliefs, demonology, and eschatology may be predicted. The early Slavs cremated their dead, sharing this custom with their other Indo-European neighbors (Lithuanians, Germans, Celts). Burial was adopted through foreign influence, and before the various conversions both customs existed side by side. The primitive pagan Slavs were animists and attributed a soul to the natural elements in which they lived. They honored a supreme deity and also believed in the existence of wood, water, and household spirits to which they offered sacrifices. Beside these nature spirits, they also honored the spirits of their ancestors and thus believed in a future life. They deified the heavenly bodies and the great phenomena of nature (thunder, lightning, wind, rain, fire).

Beside these animistic and manistic beliefs, the pagan Slavs also venerated a limited number of gods, some of which were of alien origin. The organization of a veritable pantheon was carried farthest by the Western Slavs who lived along the Baltic coast, a phenomenon perhaps not unconnected with Germanic influences of early date. It is reasonably clear that all the primitive Slavs possessed a god of the thunder and lightning, though this deity, Perun, took on special importance among the Russian Slavs because of special Scandinavian influences and the importance of Thor in the Scandinavian pantheon. Among the Western Slavs, however, Perun was less dominant than the god of the shining sun, Svarog, a name apparently connected with the indo-European base *svar*, signifying "heat,

The Primitive Slavs

brilliance." The Slavic sun god was also known as Dazhbog, the god which gives life and fertility, but neither appellation, curiously enough, appears among the Southern Slavs. Dazhbog is occasionally called the son of Svarog, the god of fire.

A more general Slavic deity was Veles or Volos. In the Russian *Primary Chronicle* he is characterized as "the god of cattle," but this qualification has no relation to the original attributes of Veles. It results rather from the monkish chronicler's identification of the specifically Russian form of his name (Volos) with that of Saint Blasius, a Cappadocian bishop who died a martyr's death about 315 A.D., and was extensively revered thereafter as a patron of flocks and herds. In the *Primary Chronicle,* where Perun and Veles are mentioned together as gods by whom the Scandinavian Varangians and the Slavs of Kiev swore, the implication is that the Varangians swore by Perun (here the equivalent of Thor) and the Slavs by Veles, who thus may be viewed as the guardian of oaths, a sort of *Zeus epiorkios.* The name Veles itself is cognate with various Lithuanian words meaning "corpse," "ghost," and "devil," so that Veles is rather to be considered as a god of the dead, a conclusion justified by his frequent invocation in various late Bohemian curses.

Idols were used by the Eastern Slavs, and the medieval German chroniclers describe sanctuaries which the Baltic Slavs erected to their gods. Of these the most celebrated was that at Arkona, on the island of Rugen, dedicated to the god Svantovit, whose statue adorned it. Svantovit seems merely a local variant of Svarog, the sun god, and various other local deities of the same type are mentioned in medieval non-Slavic sources. If the Slavs did honor a supreme deity, it is reasonably clear that he was a thunder or a sun god like Perun or Svarog, who would thus reflect the more or less general Indo-European belief in such a deity who appears as Zeus, Jupiter, or the old Germanic Tiuz. Only among the Baltic Slavs is the existence of a special caste of priests attested.

A final and equally interesting problem connected with the

primitive culture of the Slavs is a determination of the epoch at which they learned to write. While there have been some fruitless though entertaining attempts both at the forgery of specifically Slavic runes and at the identification as genuinely Slavic of certain Runic texts more probably of north Germanic origin, it is on the whole unlikely that letters of any sort were known in the pre-Christian period apart from cases where a more or less educated Slav managed to write down a name or a few phrases of his language in Latin or Greek characters.

II

The Slavic Migrations

We have seen that there is no evidence that the Slavs or any part of them were present in the middle or lower Danube basin before the Christian era. The Gothic historian Jordanes, writing in 551 A.D., reports that in his day the Slavs were occupying the whole valley of the lower Danube from its junction with the Save river to the sea, and that they extended east as far as the Dniester and north to the Vistula. On the basis of this passage historians have frequently maintained that the Slavs did not reach the Danube valley until the migratory Germanic tribes had evacuated both Germany and Hungary, but that their movement was so rapid that they overran this area as soon as its previous occupants had left it. Since the Byzantine historian Procopius associates the arrival of the Slavs in the Balkans with the accession of the Emperor Justinian in 521, it was easy to conclude that the Slavic movement southward began about this date.

There are, however, grounds to believe that the Slavic march toward and across the Danube was a process of longer duration, and actually began considerably earlier. It may be recalled that those tremendous movements known as the barbarian migrations started in the first century A.D. Numerous Germanic tribes made their way from eastern Germany through the Sudeten defiles into Moravia even before the year 200. These shifts of population are explicable by the pressure not only of the Lombards and the Goths, but also of the Slavs, and after the Goths reached the Black Sea during the third century, the Slavs were doubtless the chief impelling factor in such migratory movements. That the Slavic expansion was by no means a brief and spatially limited process is borne out by the fact that in the sixth century we find the Slavs already settled from the Elbe and the Saale in the west to the Don in the east, and from the Baltic in the north to the Adriatic and the Aegean in the south. They were thus occupying an area five times greater than their original home, and during the process of settlement they did not evacuate and abandon their primitive habitat, as so many German tribes (Goths, Lombards, Vandals, Burgundians) are known to have done. This fact alone indicates a slow expansion in all directions rather than a sudden shift of position.

We find in the sources some respectable evidence to support this opinion. In 448, for instance, the Emperor Theodosius II sent an embassy from Constantinople deep into Pannonia (modern Hungary) to buy off Attila and his Huns, who had recently menaced the metropolis. One member of the embassy, named Priscus, has left an account of its long and arduous journey, in the course of which he speaks of meeting in Hungary an hospitable local population whose language was not Hungarian, and who supplied a drink made of honey called *medos*. This form is probably nothing more than a Greek spelling of Old Slavonic *medŭ*, since honey beer is a traditional Slavic drink and Priscus would have written the word with an *i* if he had been talking about Gothic mead. Jordanes also mentions that the funeral of Attila was accompanied by a great feast called a *strava*, which is a well-known medieval Slavic usage, apart from the fact that the word itself is pure Slavic.

Somewhat earlier during the fourth century it is also recorded that the Sarmatians in the Hungarian plain were expelled from there by the subject rural population, who are identified soon after as Wends, that is, Slavs. Apart from these rather tenuous historical data, there are also a certain number of place names dating as far back as the second century not only in the western district between the rivers Drave and Save, but also in Hungary north of the Danube, which cannot be etymologized as anything but Slavic. It is therefore probable that some Slavic infiltration into this area began as early as the first century, and it is entirely certain that Slavs were present there between the third and the fifth centuries. We may thus conclude that the Slavs began to drift into the basins of the Danube and the Save at the very opening of the Christian era, appearing at first simply as isolated islands among an alien population. The slowness of this penetration would then explain the relatively isolated character of the early place names which reflect this drift. The Slavs did not therefore hit the Danube Valley in a sudden wave. After the first scattered settlers had arrived, the major movement set in during the third century when all populations north of the Carpathians were in a state of flux, so that by Jordanes's day (551) their occupancy of the Danube basin was an established fact of fairly long standing.

While it is not difficult to date in this fashion the arrival of the Slavs in the Danube basin, there is no evidence that they penetrated the Balkans proper before the year 500, unless we may suppose with some likelihood that isolated Slavic bands accompanied the numerous alien invaders known prior to that date. In any case, there is no question of real Slavic occupation of the Save and the Danube until the sixth century. Early in its course, when the Byzantine frontiers were being harassed by Huns, Bulgars, and Avars, the Slavs were also on the march southward, and they frequently made common cause with these invaders. Their chief center of population at this period was on the middle reaches of the Danube and in modern Walachia, but they attacked on a long front from Dalmatia to the very walls of Constantinople itself. With the Avars, energetic Turko-Tartars of Asiatic origin who had fought their way across the steppes to the Danube, they threatened the Greek peninsula, where their first occupation dates from 581.

Contemporary chroniclers report that the Slavs had by that time acquired wealth by pillage and fought even better than the regular Greek troops. On the Adriatic, they occupied the districts of Illyria, Dalmatia, and Istria early in the seventh century. Shortly afterward the Slavs on the western front (the Czechs and those on the Adriatic seaboard) overthrew the Avar hegemony and became independent, but after the Avars were thus weakened, the Slavs never menaced Constantinople again. Yet by the end of the seventh century the whole interior of the Balkan peninsula, especially Macedonia and its neighborhood, was populated by Slavs. They even took to the sea and reached Crete in 623. At the height of the Avar expansion, the Slavs had already passed through Thessaly, Epirus, and Attica, and reached the Peloponnese in 588. Here their occupation was so formidable that, for the next two centuries, a Byzantine Greek scarcely dared set foot in the southern portion of the peninsula, while in the north the Danube was never again fixed as the frontier of the Byzantine Empire after 601. On the other hand, it is not to be supposed that the Slavs were ever in the majority in Greece proper. Subject Greeks still formed the mass of the population. Were this not the case, it would be difficult to explain the eventual and rather rapid subsequent disappearance of the Slavic element south of Macedonia.

Once the Slavs were firmly established in the Balkans, they immediately became exposed to the older cultures they found there. Those on the Adriatic coast and in the western Danube basin felt the impact of Latin civilization transmitted through romanized native populations, through colonial centers, or through the cities of the seaboard. When they settled within the sphere of Greek influence, the dominant cultural pressure was Byzantine. The results of these accidents of location are still discernible in the intellectual orientation of the Balkan Slavs.

The Slavs were curiously tenacious in retaining their own language, but extremely receptive to manners and techniques transmitted to them through contact with superior cultures. When they were present in a majority, they experienced no difficulty in impressing their language on the indigenous minority, whom they Slavicized rapidly by intermarriage. The Dalmatian coast from Veglia to Ragusa experienced this evolution from the ninth to the last century. On the other hand, remnants of the old Romanized pre-Slavic population, known as Vlakhs, persist in the interior of the peninsula to the present day, especially in southern Macedonia and the Pindus, while the Romanians, in spite of Slavic and Turko-Tartar admixture, are a concentrate of Romanized pre-Slavic native elements. Of the indigenous and un-Romanized population prior to the migrations, the Thracians in the eastern half of the peninsula disappeared altogether, while the Illyrians in the western half survive fractionally as the Albanians. The linguistic differences between Serbian and Bulgarian have sometimes been explained by the existence of an Illyrian substratum in the former, and a Thracian in the latter, since the areas occupied by the new vernaculars correspond roughly to the regions occupied by these two pre-Slavic elements. Of the migrant tribes who preceded the Slavs into the Balkans no trace remains. The Celts had passed from the scene before the Slavs arrived. The Sarmatians, driven into the Balkans from the steppes, were known as early as the fourth century only by scanty place names. A few Germanic islands kept their names until the fifth century. The Huns rapidly dissolved after Attila's death, while the Avars, after the Slavs threw off their yoke, were decimated by their wars with Charlemagne before the year 800, and the remnant was absorbed by the adjacent Slavs.

Though we find in the Balkans an uninterrupted set of Slavic dialects gradually shading into each other, from the Adriatic to the Black Sea, the three basic literary languages (Slovenian, Serbo-Croatian, and Bulgarian) are well-differentiated vernaculars. It is not to be supposed, however, that this differentiation originated after the dispersion. On the contrary it may be assumed that the germs of dialectal differentiation inherent in the proto-Slavic language even at the epoch of closest ethnic unity evolved into more conspicuous local characteristics as the race gradually spread. It seems probable that the sections of the proto-Slavs whose vernaculars were the precursors of the present South Slavonic languages were geographically placed in their original habitat in an order corresponding to their present locations. The Slovenes are the furthest northwest of the modern South Slavs. It would appear, then, that their proto-Slavic ancestors lived in the southwest corner of the proto-Slavic habitat on the upper Vistula. Similarly, the ancestors of the Serbo-Croatians must have lived in the vicinity of the central Carpathians (there is, in fact, some etymological relationship between the words *Carpathian* and *Croatian*). The proto-Bulgars lived further eastward and seem to have descended the Prut and the Seret rivers toward the lower Danube while the western proto-Slavs came through the Sudeten passes into Bohemia and Moravia.

The forefathers of the Slovenes, after crossing the Danube soon after the beginning of the Christian era, first appear in history after 592, when they attacked the cities of Istria and northern Italy and made war against the Duke of Bavaria in modern Styria. They were dominated by the Avars early in the seventh century, and after the Avars were dispersed fell first under Bavarian and then (788) under Frankish sovereignty. Then as now their settlement was most dense in southern Styria, Carinthia, and Carniola, though their zone of occupation contracted appreciably under German pressure as time went on so that the northern Slovenian border was pushed south from the Danube to the Drave.

The Croatians and Serbs make their appearance in the western half of the Balkan peninsula south of the Slovenes somewhat earlier than the historical debut of the latter. They were thus reported along the coast at Salona in 536 and at Durazzo in 548. Their starting point was apparently the Vistula valley, though in their migrations they left important remnants in Silesia and the Riesengebirge which made their presence felt in local place names before they were assimilated by other Slavic elements of these areas. On the other hand, materials dealing with the early existence of the Serbo-Croats on the Balkan peninsula are strikingly scanty. Both assume historical importance only in the ninth century, when the Serbs collided with the Bulgars and the Croats with other Slavs and with Franks in the middle Danube basin.

The destiny of the Slavs in modern Bulgaria was subject to influences differing radically from that of their kindred in the western Balkans. The territory which they had occupied in the sixth century was traversed several times during the seventh century by a nation of Turko-Tartar invaders known as the Bulgars, who had come into the Balkans from across the steppe country, but at first retired behind the Danube after each of their incursions southward. About 670, however, when other powerful Turkic elements began to occupy the south Russian prairies and coastline, they were obliged to seek a residence in the Danube delta and south of it. They thus settled down in Moesia, the flat country between the Danube and the chains of mountains further south. During this process, they seem to have arrived without difficulty at an understanding with the Slavic residents, whose local princes became subject to the Bulgar khan. But here, as elsewhere, it was the invaders who were culturally assimilated. The Bulgars abandoned their own idiom for Slavic, and while Bulgars and Slavs were still differentiated in this area during the eighth century, they were viewed as identical in the ninth. It is thus clear that numerically the Slavs in Moesia must have been more numerous than the energetic and warlike Bulgars whose name they adopted. The new Bulgarian state rapidly expanded its influence to include Macedonia even down to Salonika and the Aegean coast.

The Slavic flood which overwhelmed the Greek peninsula in the last twenty years of the sixth century lasted until about

800, but in the next two hundred years Byzantine authority was gradually reëstablished throughout Hellas proper. By the twelfth century, in fact, there were but scattered Slavic remnants to be found south of Epirus and Thessaly. Though place names still yield abundant traces of this Slavic occupation, historians have long since disproved the famous thesis of Fallmerayer that the race of the ancient Greeks had been annihilated in Europe. As a matter of fact, as soon as Byzantine supremacy was restored, what Slavs there were throughout the countryside became assimilated so fast that they disappeared altogether. In Macedonia, on the other hand, though Greek civilization tended to recover and even to dominate as time progressed, the local Slavs were still numerous enough to preserve their ethnic and linguistic identity. In Hellas, however, the native Greek element was too populous and the Slavic colonists too few to make such a survival possible. Somewhat the same situation prevailed further north in Transylvania and Walachia, where the Slavic settlers eventually faded out under Romanian pressure.

While the problems connected with the migrations and the settlement of the Southern Slavs are relatively simple, if we except the alien influences affecting the Bulgarians and the decline of Slavic domination in Hellas, the destinies of the Western Slavs are, for a variety of reasons, infinitely more complex. At the beginning of the Christian era the whole expanse of northern Europe from the Rhine to the Vistula and from the Baltic, first to the Sudetens and later to the Danube, was occupied by Germanic tribes. From the second to the fifth centuries, certain important Germanic units moved out of the basins of the Elbe, the Oder, and their confluents, so that by the fourth century eastern Germany was almost totally evacuated by its Germanic inhabitants. Though German savants have been traditionally loth to admit that there were any Slavs in this area during the first period of German settlement, there are a number of tribal names which the classical historians for lack of accurate knowledge bulked with the Germans,

The Slavic Migrations 35

but which justify the hypothesis that there were at least some Slavic elements west of the Vistula in classical premigration times. Hence, the westward Slavic drift very likely began sometime before the Slavs actually appear on the Oder and the Elbe in the fifth century A.D.

Even with the Germanic tribes present, the area was sparsely enough settled, and it is illogical to suppose that this district was totally denuded of human habitation when they left to pursue their destinies elsewhere. Archaeologically, Germanic civilization comes to an abrupt halt in eastern Germany during the fourth century. Furthermore since the proto-Slavs had a chance to adopt the types of Roman provincial pottery, they must have begun to spread toward the Roman outposts before that date. It would, on the other hand, take us too far afield to belabor the point whether or not the Slavs were in German territory before the Germans descended from Scandinavia. We may thus limit ourselves to the admission that there were some Slavic elements in eastern Germany west of the Vistula even when this area was under German occupation before the migrations began, and the Slavs may well have been the *superiores barbari* who, according to Julius Capitolinus, set so many Germanic tribes in motion during the reign of Marcus Aurelius.

But even if we thus suppose that the Slavs crossed the Vistula before 150 A.D., their occupation of Germany to the Elbe and the Oder is not historically confirmed until early in the sixth century. In 512 Procopius mentions that the Germanic Heruli, after defeat by the Lombards, made their way north to Denmark "through all the nations of the Sclaveni," and the Elbe and the Saale are elsewhere mentioned at the same period as the frontier between German and Slav. Apprehensive of Slavic penetration west of this line, Charlemagne in 805 fixed the Slavic boundary, the *limes sorabicus,* running roughly northward from Regensburg to the Saale and from the vicinity of Magdeburg northwestward across country to the estuary of the Elbe and the site of modern Hamburg. The border was later continued on a line roughly connecting the sites of Hamburg and Kiel. South of Hamburg there were actual Slavic survivals almost into the nineteenth century, that is until 1798.

In an area including not only the whole of Germany east of the Elbe and the entire extent of pre-Hitler Czechoslovakia and Poland, important linguistic differentiations are inevitable. The Czech or Czechoslovak language developed in the upper basins of the Elbe and the Oder, and is especially notable for the fixation of the accent on the first syllable. While the variations of Slovak from Czech are doubtless of early origin, they were intensified by the comparative isolation of the Slovaks at some distance to the east on the edge of Hungary and, in more recent times, by close contacts between Slovaks on one hand and Magyars and South Slavs on the other. Another Western Slavic dialect, Sorabic or Sorbic, which also has a fixed accent on the first syllable, evolved in close proximity to Czech, but is in a sense a transitional dialect between Polish and Czech. This language survives only as spoken by some one hundred thousand people in a small area known as Lausitz, or Lusatia, on the Spree northeast of Dresden. A third dialect, Polabic (that is, the language of the Slavs on the Elbe, or Laba), along with Pomeranian, was spoken in the coastal area between Hamburg and the mouth of the Vistula. Of Polabic no vestiges remain, and there is some doubt whether Pomeranian, now represented only by the Kashubic survivors west of Danzig, is not more properly a northern Polish dialect. And finally, the Polish language evolved in the basins of the upper Oder and the Vistula.

With the exception of the numerically unimportant surviving descendants of the Pomeranians and the Sorbs (Kashubs and Lusatians), all Western Slavs in the Elbe basin and on the Baltic disappeared in the German movement of eastward colonization which began under Charlemagne. In spite of heroic efforts by medieval Slavic princelings to make a firm stand against the great Germanic empire supported by the Roman church, none of these Slavs escaped the German yoke later

The Slavic Migrations

than 1167, and long before that date the process of extermination or assimilation had set in.

In view of the latest developments in modern history, let us pause a moment on the origins of the Czechoslovaks. The primeval habitat of Czechs and Slovaks was located north of the Carpathians between the headwaters of the Oder and the middle Vistula. The Czechs reached Bohemia and Moravia by the upper reaches of the Neisse and Oder and westward through the Sudeten range and between the Gesenke and the Jablunka. The Slovaks, on the other hand, arrived in their present location between the Morava and the Danube by passing the western Carpathians (that is, the Beskids and the High Tatra south of modern Krakow). The western limits of the Czechs were thus the Böhmer Wald and the Erzgebirge, while on the north they enjoyed a good natural frontier in the mountains from the Sudetens to the Carpathians. On the south the Bohemians and Moravians originally extended to the Danube, but were gradually pushed back along the river between Linz and Vienna until the twelfth century, though the Slovaks maintained contact with it at Bratislava (Pressburg). The western Slovak limit is still roughly the river Morava, which joins the Danube about thirty miles east of Vienna.

There is no longer much question but that the Czech and the Slovak languages were originally an identical dialect just as their speakers were primitively one group, but even in modern times there is an appreciable diversity of dialect, culture, and character among various sections of even the Czechs themselves, and the present differentiation of the Slovaks was conditioned and intensified by geographical separation from the Czechs and by the long-standing political dominance of the Magyars since 1029. The intellectual gap between Czech and Slovak is also due to the rapid Czech assimilation of German culture. Finally, at the extreme east end of the state of Czechoslovakia is an area known as Subcarpathian Russia. Its inhabitants speak a Ukrainian (Little Russian) dialect perfectly distinct from either Czech or Slovak. They are thus not Western Slavs at all, like their Czech and Slovak neighbors, but descendants of South Russian tribes which retired into the mountains from the basins of the Bug and the Dniester to escape the inroads of Turko-Tartar nomads who swarmed across the steppe country in the course of the eleventh and twelfth centuries.

Curiously enough, the early history of the Poles is more obscure than that of any other Slavic group, though they still inhabit primitive Slavic territory and their language provides ample evidence of their affiliation with the Western Slavs. Originally they were not as numerous a nation as they now appear, but simply a complex of small tribes, one of which, the Polyane, gradually expanded and subjected the rest. Even the Russian *Primary Chronicle,* that eleventh century narrative which is the principal source for the traditional and legendary early habitat of the Slavs along the Danube, divides the Poles (whom it calls Lyakhs) into two large tribes, the Polyane (Polyanians) and the Mazovians. The Polyanians were the Slavs who inhabited the flat country (or *pole*) on both sides of the Warta river, a district of which modern Poznań (Pozen) would be about the center. Their northern limit was the river Notecz, or Netze, because to the north, between this river and the Baltic, lived the Pomeranians, between modern Stettin and Danzig. Their western boundary was the middle Oder at Frankfurt and the Bober. The Mazovians inhabited the Vistula basin west of modern Warsaw. Various minor tribes of less numerical consequence were later absorbed when the Polish state began to form during the tenth century. Beside Poznań, Gniezno (also in Polyanian territory) was one of the earliest Polish civic centers. The differentiation between Lyakhs and Polyanians is believed to rise from the fact that, if etymology is any guide, the former inhabited untilled land and were therefore shepherds, hunters, and trappers, while the Polyanians, as their name implies, were cultivators and farmers. The eastern boundary of the Poles in their earliest national life would not

The Slavic Migrations 39

seem to have differed greatly from the demarcation line established by the Russo-German agreement of 1939 and extending south from East Prussia to the west of Brest-Litovsk and on to the river San in Galicia. As far as the former "Corridor" is concerned, there is no early evidence whatever that the medieval Poles as such ever extended to the seacoast.

Before their expansion the original home of the Eastern Slavs, forefathers of the Russians, included the basin of the Pripet River, and further eastward, those of the rivers Berezina and Desna, the first of which flows into the Dnieper from the northeast above the confluence of the Pripet, while the Desna joins the Dnieper from the east just north of modern Kiev. The East Slavic area probably included all of Volhynia as well. The Eastern Slavs thus did not cling to the slopes of the Carpathians and even in their earliest recognizable stages covered a larger area than any of their kindred. This area was, moreover, particularly favorable to further expansion. The Desna flows far eastward into central Russia, where its headwaters lie close to those of the Oka, a tributary of the Volga. The sources of the Dnieper itself are separated by easy portages from those of western Dvina, which empties into the gulf of Riga, and of the Lovat, which connects through Lake Ilmen with the Volkhov, which in turn flows into Lake Ladoga. This lake itself is connected with the Finnish gulf by the Neva River. The headwaters of the Seim, a branch of the Desna, approach those of the Donetz and the Don, while the Dnieper in turn was an ancient and important route southward to the Black Sea. To the west, the Pripet and its branches offer easy access to the Niemen and the Vistula. There are in this area no insurmountable natural barriers, and the rivers offer a far-flung network of easy communications in all directions.

The expansion of the Eastern Slavs depended not only on these factors, but also on the circumstance that to the east and northeast they met no serious opposition, for the Finnish tribes who resided there were scattered and offered little resistance. The early Thracian and Iranian neighbors of the Eastern Slavs (first the Cimmerians, then the Scythians and the Sarmatians) succumbed to the Gothic hegemony, which was broken by the Hunnish attack of 370 A.D. The Huns were the precursors of a long series of Turko-Tartar invaders who crossed the steppes in historical times and offered a succession of recurrent barriers to any large-scale and enduring East Slavic migration toward the Black Sea. The Huns were followed in the sixth century by the Avars, who did not remain long in the steppes, but pushed on into the Danube basin where we have already met them as allies and later masters of the Danubian Slavs during the migration period.

While the Avars were sowing destruction along the northern border of the Byzantine empire, a new Turkic power was rising between the Don and the Volga. The immense Turkic agglomeration, which extended in the late sixth century from Mongolia to the Sea of Azov, had divided into two parts, eastern and western. The center of the western section was located on the lower Volga, and its prince or khan was inferior in standing only to the Great Khan of the eastern Turks. To the inhabitants of this western Turkic state, the name Khazars was given by the Armenians, from whom the Byzantines borrowed it.

During the Avar disturbances along the Danube and in the Balkans at the end of the sixth century, the remnants of the Hunnish and Bulgar tribes (both Turko-Tartar) east of the Don had restored some semblance of union and developed for a brief period into an ambitious state. The power of the Avars was concentrated far to the west and exercised only an inefficient control over their eastern marches. One active Bulgarian princeling named Kubrat applied for Byzantine aid in casting off the Avar yoke and apparently received this support at the price of his conversion to Christianity. At his death in 642, Kubrat had come to rule over a broad territory known as Great Old Bulgaria, which extended from the lower Don down to the Kuban district in the northern Caucasus. After the demise of Kubrat, his realm fell a prey to the energetic Turks who were

The Slavic Migrations 41

destined to develop the Khazar state. The advance of the Khazars inspired a wide dispersion of the Bulgars. One branch recrossed the Don and, continuing northward, eventually settled near the junction of the Volga and the Kama, where they appear in later Russian history. The other section moved westward and, after uniting with their tribal kinsmen who had preceded them into the Balkans, carried their standards to Salonika in 675 before they settled in Moesia and fused with the South Slavs already resident there. But the Khazars remained in the steppe country, and gradually spread out across the prairies until they reached the southern Bug.

From such indications as we have that the Eastern Slavs had penetrated as far east as the Sea of Azov in the sixth century, their contacts with the various waves of mobile Asiatic invaders must have been closer than the scanty data of extant sources record though, in view of the infinitely small number of Turko-Tartar loan words which found their way into the Slavic vocabulary prior to the recorded history of the Slavs, it is evident that this contact was productive of little intellectual influence on the Slavs themselves. In fact, thanks to their association with Iranian and Goth, the Eastern Slavs had attained a degree of civilization at least equal and probably superior to that of the series of Turko-Tartar nomads who traversed southern Russia between the fourth and the seventh centuries.

During this interval, in any case, the steppes between the Don and the Dnieper were the scene of constant shifts of population. Fleeing before the Huns, the Goths had moved back into central Europe. Driven by the Avars, the western Bulgars had pushed forward into the Balkans. The Avars themselves were ultimately demolished by combined Frank, Slav, and Bulgar offensives along the Danube, and the eastern Bulgar units were displaced by the Khazars. The period of Khazar expansion westward was thus an epoch peculiarly favorable for the progress of the Eastern Slavs down the valleys of the Dnieper and the Dniester. Traces of this colonization are preserved in the *Primary Chronicle,* which places the Slavic Ulichians and Tivercians between the Dnieper and the Dniester as late as the ninth century, remarking that their settlements once extended as far as the coast of the Black Sea. These are, however, the same tribes who later took refuge in the eastern Carpathians and are the ancestors of the modern inhabitants of Subcarpathian Russia. In any case, after the elimination of the Avars, the East Slavic process of southward settlement was resumed until it was once more interrupted by the passage of the Magyars across southern Russia after the middle of the ninth century, and by subsequent inroads of the Pechenegs (Patzinaks), another wave of Turko-Tartar nomads, in the tenth century. Hence, among the earliest traditions preserved in the medieval Russian annals is that the South Russian Slavic tribes were ancient Khazar tributaries. In the early ninth century these subject tribes extended up the Dnieper as far as the river Sozh, well north of Kiev, and thus brought the whole initial extent of the subsequent principality of Kiev under Khazar tutelage.

The Khazars were a progressive race capable of rapid intellectual development and avid in the absorption of foreign ideas. Despite close diplomatic relations with Byzantium, they carefully sidestepped all influence toward conversion to Christianity with its political implications. Persecutions of the Jews in Byzantium during the reign of Leo III (717-740) caused a considerable Jewish migration from the Empire to the Khazar cities around the straits of Kerch. Since these Khazar centers (Kerch and Phanagoria, together with Itil, at the mouth of the Volga) were the chief transit points for Asiatic trade with the west, the Jewish settlers found abundant scope for their innate commercial talents, and rapidly came to exert a pronounced intellectual influence which culminated in the eighth century in the conversion of the Khazar ruling classes to Judaism. A remarkable feature of the Khazar polity was its religious tolerance, which guaranteed equal privileges not only to Jew and Moslem, but also to Christian refugees fleeing the rigors of the iconoclastic movement in Byzantium itself.

The Slavic Migrations 43

Like the Scythian and Sarmatian kingdoms of which it was the functional successor, the Khazar state rested upon a fusion of agrarian and commercial interests. Its nominal ruler was the *khan* (*Khakan*), who was substantially a religious figurehead. The actual administration was in the hands of the *beg*, who commanded the standing army composed chiefly of mercenaries of Khwarizmian, Slavic, and later even of Scandinavian extraction. The Khazar capital was situated at Itil, near the site of modern Astrakhan, and in the eighth and ninth centuries Khazaria was hardly of less importance to Byzantine foreign policy than the Carolingian Empire. The Khazar domination over their northern tributaries was, however, loosely organized, and the small Khazar standing army was incapable of serious offensive operations, a weakness doubly menacing in view of the fact that the series of nomadic incursions from the plains of Asia was as yet unfinished. About 860 the Khazar state was shaken by the fierce inroads of a new Turko-Tartar tribe, the Pechenegs, who had previously dwelt between the Volga and the Yaik until set in motion by the pressure of other kindred peoples behind them. The Pechenegs drove the Magyars across the Dnieper and on into central Europe, caused a concentration of the Eastern Slavs on the middle Dnieper, and aroused such apprehension among the Khazars that the latter, to protect their interests in the steppe country, sought the aid of Byzantine engineers to construct the new fortress of Sarkel on the lower Don. From this point dates the decline of the Khazar state, which was also hastened by influences emanating from the specifically Slavic areas of the Dnieper valley. In fact the decline of Khazaria stimulated the evolution of the Kiev principate, the economic development of which stamps it as the logical heir of the Khazar polity.

The influence of the Khazars on the culture of the Eastern Slavs at the dawn of their history is greater than usually appreciated, since the Khazar dominance extended over a period of some two centuries and was the bearer of a relatively advanced civilization. In view of the fact that the Khazars are known to have kept a garrison at Kiev, it is even probable that the name of that city is of Khazar origin, that is, *küi,* "bank of a river," and *ev,* "settlement," which well accords with the lower part of the city as it still is today.

On the north and the east, the Eastern Slavs were eventually confronted by Finnish tribes. We have relatively little data on the primitive habitat of the Finns, but modern scholarship places it in the extreme eastern section of northern Europe, on the edge of the Ural mountains and even further eastward. They were thus concentrated from earliest times in the basins of the rivers Oka, the Kama, and the middle Volga, and it is from this nucleus that they spread westward to the Finnish Gulf, occupying not only Karelia and modern Finland, but also the southern shore as far as the Gulf of Riga, hence modern Esthonia and much of present-day Latvia. In central Russia their line of settlement extended as far west as modern Moscow, where they were in touch with an original Lithuanian population which has long since disappeared. Indeed, since these Lithuanian elements occupied a line running from the Baltic to the neighborhood of modern Smolensk and Kaluga, the actual contacts of Eastern Slavs and Finns cannot have begun until the Slavs themselves had already crossed the northern Dnieper and advanced toward the head of the Desna, and until the Finns themselves had begun to move westward toward the Baltic. This view is confirmed by the fact that it is only in the extreme north and east of the Russian area that Finnish linguistic influences are perceptible.

While there are some tribes known to Herodotus who may have been Finns, the Finns themselves are first mentioned with certainty by Tacitus, who did not think very highly of them, since he speaks of their remarkable ferocity at once with their sordid poverty, adding that they lived on herbs, dressed in skins, slept on the ground, and defended themselves with bone-tipped arrows. Jordanes, the Gothic historian, knew some identifiably Finnish tribes as subjects of the Goths. Our now familiar source, the Russian *Primary Chronicle,* composed after

The Slavic Migrations

the expansion of the Eastern Slavs was an accomplished fact, shows them in contact with the Finns on a long line from the Baltic to the upper Don. The chronicler distinguishes three groups of Finns: those on the Baltic, those beyond the upper Volga, and those on the middle Volga itself. The Finnish tribes south of Moscow and between Moscow and the Volga have disappeared, though the other groups are still abundantly represented even today.

Whenever the Eastern Slavs encountered the Finns, the latter either retired or remained passive. Though the Finns may have been bellicose in Tacitus's day, Jordanes knew them only as *mitissimi*—extremely pacific. In these early days the Finns showed no tendency toward urban concentration or to union for defense, while the Slavs, during the period in which their greatest expansion at Finnish expense took place (the ninth and tenth centuries), were already profiting by the military technique and leadership of courageous and enterprising Viking immigrants from Scandinavia.

At this date but one people of Finnish stock undertook an energetic offensive with perceptible historical results. These were the Magyars, who had already been in contact with Turko-Tartar tribes and had thus acquired some warlike talents. The Magyars are related to certain still extant Finnish tribes (the Voguls and the Ostyaks) on the river Ob in Siberia. After splitting off from the ethnic nucleus in about the seventh century, they moved west into southern Russia, where they met the Khazars on the Don. Then, around 860, they pushed on into Moldavia, and finally, after various raids into Pannonia and the Balkans, settled down in the Hungarian plain, where their descendants have lived since about the year 900. Their subsequent contacts were thus largely with the Southern and the Western Slavs.

None of these Finnish tribes have any ethnic or linguistic relationship with the Slavic tribes. But with the Lithuanians the situation is somewhat different. The Lithuanians are an Indo-European people, and their language shows affinity with

Slavonic, although the two idioms have undergone widely variant evolutions over a long period. It is generally held by competent scholars that there was at some early date an epoch of Balto-Slavic unity. Precisely when this unity existed it is not so easy to say. The facts that certain Iranian words appear in Slavic without a counterpart in Lithuanian, and that the Balts borrowed other words from Finnish which the Slavs do not possess, have given rise to the theory that the Balts and the Slavs had separated before the arrival of the Scythians and even early in the bronze age, hence before 1000 B.C. But these are very tenuous proofs, and the most we can say with certainty is that the Balts and the Slavs had been separated for a long time before history knew either of them.

The modern extent of Lithuanian (Baltic) territory in Lithuania, Latvia, and their environs is, moreover, much more limited than it was in an earlier age, for before the westward migration of the Finns from the Volga, the Letto-Lithuanian people occupied the Baltic coast from the Vistula to the Gulf of Finland and the interior across White Russia (Byelorussia) to the western limit of the Finns between the upper Volga and Moscow rivers north of the line of settlement of the early Eastern Slavs. There were Lithuanian survivals, a tribe known as the Galindians, near Moscow as late as the thirteenth century, showing that Slavic colonization in central Russia encountered not only Finns, but also Balts. The Russian *Primary Chronicle* thus knows not only the Galindians, but also the Prussians on the coast east of the Vistula, and the Lithuanians (a specific tribal name) and other Baltic units around the Gulf of Riga where the Letts now reside. It should be noted that the German Prussians derive their name from the old home of the Lithuanian Prussians, that is, modern East Prussia, the country south of Danzig and Königsberg. This area was subjugated by the Teutonic knights during the thirteenth century, after which the eradication of the original Baltic inhabitants proceeded so rapidly that the language had died out by the year 1700.

The Slavic Migrations

It was necessary to dwell at some length on the contacts of the Eastern Slavs because the area which they inhabit is, after all, fairly remote, and the process by which they came to occupy it is likewise far from the ken of any but the specialist. As the Eastern Slavs branched out into the steppes toward the Black Sea and the Don and northeastward at the expense of Lithuanian and Finnish tribes, the old unity tended to relax in proportion to their dispersion. New centers of population formed at considerable distances from the old foci. The colonizers underwent new influences which varied with their locations. The southeastern settlers experienced Khazar influence, the northern colonies were close to Scandinavia of the Viking age, and the Slavs along the lower Dnieper were within the cultural sphere of Byzantium.

The Arabic geographers who described eastern Europe of the ninth century already noted four centers of Eastern Slavic concentration at that early period: one near Lake Ilmen, another on the Oka River near the city of Ryazan, one at Kiev, and a fourth in Galicia, and more detailed tribal designations among the Eastern Slavs were likewise known to both German and Greek sources of the same period. Finally, the oft-cited Russian *Primary Chronicle* preserves from traditions considerably earlier than the twelfth century not only a list of tribes on Russian soil, but also their locations. These tribes are the Croats, the Polyane, the Volhynians, the Dulebians, the Buzhane, the Dregovichians, the Polotians, the Novgorod Slavs, the Severians, the Krivichians, the Radimichians, the Vyatichians, the Ulichians, and the Tivercians.

The Croats mentioned were a remnant of the tribe of the same name which remained behind in eastern Galicia, Bukovina, and on the Prut and the Dniester rivers after others of their kindred had moved on into the Balkans. The Dulebians, the Volhynians, and the Buzhane (who are connected by their name with the river Bug in Volhynia) inhabited Volhynia in the neighborhood of modern Lutsk. The Derevlians (whose name is connected with Slavic *derevo*, "wood"), occupied the vast forests south of the Pripet River, and were, on account of their remote location, culturally backward.

In this respect, they contrast with their eastern neighbors, the Polyane, who lived in the prairie country (their name characterizes them as plain dwellers) on the west bank of the Dnieper north and south of the ancient city of Kiev, which had been a point of settlement since far back into the stone age. It is not unlikely that the metropolis mentioned by the geographer Ptolemy in the second century and the *Danparstathir* of Gothic tradition and the Norse *Hervárarsága* were settlements on the site of modern Kiev. Situated on a strategic trade route, the Polyane were exposed to the stimulating influences of both Scandinavian and Byzantine culture as the power of the Khazars waned. It is thus by no means accidental that their chief center became the nucleus toward which adjacent tribes gravitated and that center from which foreign culture radiated throughout the entire period before it was sacked by the Tartars in 1240.

The Ulichians and the Tivercians, the ancestors of the present inhabitants of Subcarpathian Russia, present a more complicated problem. According to the *Primary Chronicle*, they lived on the southern Bug and the Dniester, extending down to the Black Sea coast and as far as the Danube. They are without question the Eastern Slavic tribes which progressed the farthest toward the sea but, because of that same fact, they also occupied a position critically exposed to repeated nomad attacks. They can therefore hardly have moved south until after the departure of the Avars in the sixth century, and they were seriously menaced again by the incursion of the Magyars in the ninth century. We know from Arabic sources that the Magyars even enslaved much of the Slavic population in this area. Then, in the early tenth century, nomad incursions so increased in intensity and frequency that peaceful habitation in the coastal area eventually became impossible. The Ulichians and the Tivercians thus withdrew to the Carpathians and provided an important center of Slavic settlement in Tran-

The Slavic Migrations 49

sylvania and northern Hungary. This settlement did not take place, however, until after the tenth century, so that the Subcarpathian Russians actually did not come to occupy their present seats until some five hundred years after the dispersion of the proto-Slavs. There are, indeed, numerous place names even in the interior of Hungary which, by their Slavic origin, bear witness to the movement of these tribes.

The easternmost of the East Slavic tribes on Russian soil were the Severians. Though placed by the *Primary Chronicle* on the Desna and its eastern tributaries, they seem to have constituted the Slavic element which pushed as far east as the Don river in the sixth century and are even located by ninth-century Arab geographers on the lower Volga and in the northern Caucasus. But, like the Ulichians and the Tivercians, they too were exposed to Turko-Tartar impacts which drove them back to the region between modern Kursk, in the north-central Ukraine, and the left bank of the Dnieper. Their chief cities were Chernigov, on the Desna, and Pereslavl, southeast of Kiev on the left bank of the Dnieper.

North of the Derevlians, between the Pripet and the Dvina and as far east as the Berezina, lived the Dregovichians. Their area of occupation corresponds fairly closely to the modern White-Russian (Byelorussian) district, and thus would border on the zone of Lithuanian occupation. In fact, they are the Slavic group responsible for the contraction of this zone, since they pushed the Lithuanians back toward the Baltic coast and settled the basins of the Dvina and the Niemen rivers. Their chief cities were Turov, on the Pripet, and Pinsk, east of modern Brest-Litovsk. While their tribal appellation has been quite naturally connected with a word for marsh, it is, because of its termination *-ich,* more likely a patronymic.

To the east of the Berezina and straddling the Dnieper, the Radimichians were an unimportant and backward tribe which fell comparatively early under the sway of Kiev. Further east, even as far as the Oka River and modern Moscow, and thus on the edge of the eastern Finns, lived the Vyatichians, who were early colonizers in territory originally Finnish. The same observation applies to the Slovenes or Novgorod Slavs about Lake Ilmen, who thus approach the region of the great lakes. Just why they alone preserved the ethnic name of the Slavs remains an enigma. At any rate, they were, with the Polyane of Kiev, the most progressive of the Eastern Slavs. Located in an area ill-fitted for agriculture, they lived by hunting and trapping, by which they acquired material for barter with Scandinavian traders. Their pioneering spirit gradually carried them still further north toward Lakes Ladoga and Onega, and since only a short portage separated them from the upper Volga, we eventually find them pushing southeastward to insure a food supply from the grain fields of the Moscow district. They founded the city of Novgorod where the Volkhov flows out of Lake Ilmen, and economic and political collisions between this city and Moscow were a familiar feature of later medieval Russian history until the Muscovites emerged as victors.

Just south of the Slovenes lived the Krivichians, who dominated the headwaters of the Dvina, Dnieper, and Volga rivers and extended northwest until they collided with the Balts and Finns in the neighborhood of modern Pskov. Their chief centers, both of which owed their importance to river traffic, were Polotzk on the Dvina and Smolensk on the upper Dnieper. Since Smolensk is situated at an easy portage point between the Dvina, Lovat, and Dnieper rivers, it was one of the earliest points of Scandinavian settlement in the interior of Russia.

It stands to reason that, at the dawn of Russian history, these tribes must have in many instances progressed far beyond any patriarchal organization on the basis of kinship. Essentially an agricultural people, yet living also by hunting and trapping in newly colonized and sparsely settled areas, the Russian Slavs tended to develop beyond a purely patriarchal society as soon as they came to inhabit small farms grouped about a fortified village which served as a focal point for defense and as a rudimentary market for the exchange of their products. Such of these villages as were located on the chief watercourses developed into genuine trading posts and towns, the importance of which was enhanced by the penetration of foreign merchants at the beginning of the historical period. The rise of trading posts and towns gradually concentrated adjacent agricultural areas under the control of the former, producing at the same time accumulations of wealth in the hands of a new ruling class which appropriated to itself the influence formerly wielded by the elders of family, clan, and tribe. The growing prestige of the towns also broke down the various tribal differentiations, since portions of the same tribal area might fall for reasons of geography and communication under the control of different towns.

In general, the Russian tribes formed three groups distinguishable by their speech, which are reflected in our day by the tripartite division of the Russian language into three basic dialects. The northern group, comprising the Slovenes (Slavs) of Novgorod and the Krivichians, is the forerunner of the modern Great Russian dialect, the standard literary language. The central group, including Dregovichians, Radimichians, Vyatichians, and Severians, divided into two sections, of which the eastern joined the northern, or ultimately Great Russian element, while the western section (Dregovichians, Radimichians) came to form the White Russian element centering around Minsk. The southern group, made up of Polyane, Derevlians, Volhynians, Ulichians, Tivercians, and Croats, evolved into the Little Russian or Ukrainian element. In fact, the term *Ukraina* goes back as far as at least 1187, and means the southern border district. The differences among these three dialects have of course been intensified as time went on by the accidents of political affiliation and by diversified cultural influences. But these three groups are none the less parts of the same nation, so that either a White Russian or a Ukrainian is precisely as much a Russian as the purest Great Russian born in the shadow of the Kremlin.

III

Conversion and Religious Divisions

While conversion to Christianity was an inevitable phase of the process by which the Slavs were drawn into the general movement of European civilization, it was by no means an unmixed blessing. When Slavic tribes had evolved to some semblance of national consciousness and even statehood, or were sufficiently remote from the center where religious influence was exempt from political pressure, they were able to retain their independence and to follow a characteristic course of development. But if they lived on the periphery of a powerful and aggressive Christian state, their political independence was frequently threatened, and if this state cherished colonial aims, the convert Slavs were very likely to face the choice between assimilation and enslavement, or, at the very worst, complete extermination.

The section of the medieval church which brought about the conversion was also a factor of durable historical weight. The Western Church was devoted to the tradition of Latin culture. It insisted on the celebration of the Mass in the hallowed language of the Church. Hence it evinced little concern for the creation of any vernacular culture. Though not possessed of the same vitality, the Eastern Church soon found that it could evangelize the various pagans on the long Byzantine frontier more effectively if it allowed them to use their native languages in the service. Hence, though much of early south or east Slavic literature is either translated or imitated, the fact remains that the Slavs under Byzantine intellectual and religious influence developed significant national cultures much more rapidly than those under the domination of Rome. That these cultures, after a brilliant initial spurt, were later retarded and even brought to a halt which lasted several centuries is due, not to the source of conversion itself, but to historical accidents which supervened after conversion took place. Had not the Eastern and the Southern Slavs fallen victims, in one case to Tartar invasion and in the other to Turkish conquest, their intellectual lag in comparison with the rest of Europe would not have been so great. The Russians, for example, were completely deprived of all Western stimulation after the middle of the thirteenth century and nearly three hundred years elapsed before they entered upon the difficult process of assimilating the Western culture which had developed during that long and critical interval. The South Slavs, on the other hand, shook off the Turkish yoke only within the last century and thus were even more handicapped than the Russians in their struggle to catch up with the modern world.

Of all the Slavs, the Slovenes in Carinthia and Carniola were the first to encounter missionary activities. Early in the seventh century, they had been temporarily combined with Czechs and Sorbs north of the Danube in the semilegendary kingdom under Samo, who led them victoriously against the Avars and simultaneously offered a temporary barrier to Frankish expansion southward. During his declining years in Switzerland, Saint Columban, the great Irish missionary, had thought, as early as 612, of setting out from Bregenz on a mission to the nearest Slavs, but, finding the task too difficult for his advanced age (he was already sixty-nine), he retired to Italy and ended his days at Bobbio.

After Samo disappeared from the scene and his realm was dissolved, the Slovenes were unable to withstand the Avars, who soon held the Danube as far as the Enns. The Slovenes then applied for aid to the Bavarians. The latter beat off the Avars, but in 750 also seized control of Styria, Carinthia, and Carniola. Then, in 788, when Charlemagne deposed Duke Tassilo of Bavaria, all Bavarian dependencies fell under the sway of the Carolingian realm. Even before this date, some of the local Slovene nobility had been converted to Christianity and consequently intermarried with Bavarian families. A number of churches had thus been founded in this area by missionaries from Salzburg, and a considerable proportion of the local Slovene population had also been Christianized before the epoch of Carolingian sovereignty.

When this sovereignty became established, missionary activities were intensified. During the reign of Charlemagne there were two centers from which missionary activity reached the Slovenes: the archbishopric of Salzburg and the patriarchate of Aquileia, at the head of the Adriatic. The former soon took the lead, and after Charlemagne defeated and dispersed the Avars in 796, the area between the Danube and the Theiss which they evacuated was added to the diocese of Salzburg. Bavarian missionaries accompanied German colonists into this district, where the new Slavic occupants were rapidly converted and Germanized, especially as the Slavic landlords were rapidly eliminated. The first bishop regularly assigned to the Slovenes was Deodoricus, ordained at Salzburg in 799. His diocese extended to the river Drave, which was the dividing line between the sees of Salzburg and Aquileia.

Similar missionary activity was also set in motion among the neighboring Croats south and east of the Slovenes. As the power of the Byzantine empire declined, the Frankish power gradually extended to the Slavs of the Adriatic coastline, so that the Dalmatian Croats were subject to the Franks from 803, and Frankish authority was but little impaired by the revolt of the Croat prince Lyudevit against Louis the Pious from 819 to 822. A few years later, for political reasons, an inland Croat district headed by Margrave Pribina, a Frankish feudatory with his headquarters in Pannonia near Lake Balaton, experienced a period of intense missionary activity stimulated by its chief. Pribina thus entered into the good graces of King Louis the German, and in 850 the archbishop of Salzburg consecrated the first Christian church in Pribina's dominions at Mosaburg, on Lake Balaton. Since fully half the notables present on this occasion bore German names, it is clear how intense German immigration had been and how far the policy of Germanization pursued by the Bavarian missionaries had proceeded. Within fifteen years Pribina's territory contained more than thirty-two churches and many monasteries. On the other hand, conversion and colonization also contributed to diminishing the area occupied by pure Slavic populations, and the rapid contraction of Slovene and Croat territory southward from the Danube is due primarily to this process.

After the dissolution of Samo's kingdom about 650, the Western Slavs in modern Czechoslovak territory played no role in history until Charlemagne's campaigns against the Avars one hundred forty years later. On these campaigns the emperor's troops passed through Bohemia, and since the pagan Slavs of this area threatened the flank of the empire, they were subjected to Frankish attacks after the year 800. Louis the Pious already possessed numerous Bohemian vassals, and in 845 fourteen Czech chieftains appeared in Regensburg at the court of Louis the German to request baptism. Somewhat further eastward, the kindred Moravians were united under one prince, Mojmir, who, though still a pagan, was also a vassal of Louis the German and thus did not oppose the operations of missionaries from Regensburg and Passau.

When Mojmir died in 845, Louis chose as the prince's successor the latter's nephew Rostislav, whom he regarded as stupid and who, he hoped, would be grateful for this elevation. Rostislav proved to be neither. Not only did he pursue Mojmir's consolidation tactics, but, while letting his allies, the disunited Czech tribes, fight against the Franks, he still maintained outward loyalty to Louis and actively promoted a policy of Christianization, hoping that a common faith would eventually combine all neighboring Slavic tribes under his sway. This ingenious policy soon worried Louis to the point where he sent a Bavarian force against Rostislav in 855, at the same time detailing another detachment to prevent the Czechs from helping him. This punitive expedition was a failure. Rostislav chased the Bavarians out of his territory and became virtually independent. The next few years were too full of complications in the west to allow Louis the luxury of reprisals against Rostislav, who extended his sway along the Danube at the expense of the disorganized Avars, and finally, in 860, deposed the Croat Prince Pribina in favor of the latter's son Kotzel. Since Pribina was loyal to Louis the German, this exploit was carried out under the pretext of making common cause with Louis' rebellious son Carloman, margrave of the Ostmark, who hoped to gain the empire with Slavic support.

In any case, Rostislav was at this juncture the independent chief of a large group of Slavic tribes, not only in Moravia but also south of the Danube. He could not be certain that Carloman, if successful, would deal any more gently with him than did Louis the German. Rostislav's expansion along the Danube had brought him into direct touch with the Bulgarians who, under the Khagan Krum before 814 and his successor Omurtag thereafter, had become a pagan state important enough to maintain diplomatic relations with both Franks and Byzantines. The Bulgarians supported Louis the German against Carloman, and Boris, their prince since 852, was now toying with the possibility of accepting conversion from Byzantium. Rostislav himself had succeeded reasonably well with the political emancipation of his countrymen. What more natural than that he should also seek their religious autonomy by creating a clergy who could use the vernacular, and would perhaps wield the book more efficiently than the sword? For the priests and monks from Salzburg and Passau were at least as good soldiers as they were clerics—the church militant in person.

Rostislav thus seems to have thought of Slavic-speaking mis-

Conversion and Religious Divisions

sionaries as early as 860. There is good evidence that he first applied to Rome in vain. After this failure, he turned to Constantinople, with enormous consequences for the future of Slavic civilization, not so much in his own domains, but throughout eastern Europe and the Balkans. Confronted, after the defeat of Carloman, by a new alliance between Louis the German and Boris of Bulgaria, Rostislav was now so placed that any political contact with the Greek empire, such as might result from closer religious affiliations, could be regarded only as eminently desirable insurance.

A Moravian mission sent by Rostislav reached Constantinople toward the end of 862 and stayed there the rest of the winter. The Eastern empire had been ruled since 843 by Michael III, picturesquely nicknamed the Drunkard despite his military and administrative ability. The chief ecclesiastical and intellectual light of Byzantium in his day was the patriarch Photius, who had held this post since 858. From a political standpoint, the mission was successful. Boris of Bulgaria was detached from his alliance with Louis the German. But the religious results of the mission were even more striking.

At Salonika, in the ninth century the center of an area largely populated by Slavs, there was stationed a Greek *drungarios* or battalion commander of noble birth by the name of Leo. He had two sons, Constantine and Methodius. Constantine had enjoyed a liberal education, studied under Photius himself, and became a professor of philosophy, but later gave up a brilliant scholarly career for monastic orders. He was eventually sent upon a missionary journey to the Khazars, on which he was accompanied by his elder brother Methodius. Likewise well-educated, Methodius had already held the post of district governor in a Slavic-speaking area not far from Salonika, but had abandoned the civil service to become a monk on Mount Athos, which he left only for the mission to Khazaria. The two brothers returned to Constantinople from this mission late in 861, about a year before Rostislav's envoys reached there. Constantine retired to private life, while Methodius became abbot of the monastery of Polychron, in the vicinity of Mount Olympus.

The two brothers were recalled from their retirement by Michael III when Rostislav's mission asked for Slavic-speaking priests. Constantine in particular had demonstrated considerable linguistic talent on his mission to Khazaria, where he had learned Hebrew, and it is certain that both brothers spoke the Bulgarian dialect which prevailed in the environs of their native city. Upon accepting the mission, and before proceeding to Moravia, Constantine invented a Slavic alphabet, and translated into the Slavic dialect he knew a selection of passages from the Gospels.

This translation is the beginning of all Slavic literature, but the nature of the alphabet invented by Constantine is questionable. We have, as it happens, two early Slavic alphabets, the so-called Glagolitic, somewhat enigmatic in origin, and the Cyrillic, which is a combination of the Greek and Latin alphabets with some additions for specifically Slavic sounds. This latter is the ancestor of the modern Russian, Serbian, and Bulgarian scripts. On account of the difficulty of the Glagolitic, it was later supplanted in Bulgaria by the Cyrillic, which is relatively close to the Greek. On purely psychological grounds, but in utter disagreement with many much more authoritative teachers and colleagues, I believe that the priority belongs to Cyrillic, since Constantine would (I assume), if only for reasons of convenience, have used an alphabet as close as possible to the one with which he was most familiar. Then later in Moravia, when he found that the German clergy viewed with suspicion and hostility everything Greek, I believe that he devised the tricky and crabbed Glagolitic, which does not resemble Greek script at all, to disarm his opponents.

Accompanied by a few Greek priests who also knew Slavic, Constantine and Methodius arrived in Moravia during the spring of 863. They were well received by Prince Rostislav, though the local clergy from Passau and Regensburg viewed them as dangerous rivals, for these Greeks were scholars and men of action who had the advantage of speaking the local language. At first they celebrated Mass in Greek, which was as incomprehensible to the masses as the Latin of the Frankish clergy. Constantine then hastened to translate the whole service, which only added to the resentment of their competitors, despite the fact that he actually translated not the Byzantine ritual but the Latin missal. In Western eyes this was a drastic and unparalleled innovation. Whatever Rostislav's good intentions were, he was not for long in a position to support the Greeks wholeheartedly, for in the autumn of 864 he had been attacked and once more reduced to vassalage by Louis the German. Yet the mission prospered to the point where the problem of ordaining new priests presented itself. Constantine even made a visit to the son of Pribina, Prince Kotzel, on Lake Balaton, who became an enthusiastic admirer of the brothers' work and confided fifty young men to him for training.

Since it was obviously undesirable, if not impossible, for Constantine and Methodius to have their disciples ordained by the bishops of Passau or Salzburg, they decided, after three years of missionary activity, to journey to Rome, where they could obtain the endorsement of Pope Nicholas I. The brothers were by no means hostile to the Pope; on the contrary, in common with numerous other Byzantine ecclesiastics of their day, they regarded the Bishop of Rome not only as the patriarch of the West but also as the supreme head of the Church. News of their arrival in Venice inspired a special invitation from Pope Nicholas to wait upon him, but before they left Venice he died in November 867 and was succeeded a month later by Adrian II. Though the Frankish opposition to the Slavic liturgy had been transmitted to the Roman clergy, Adrian ordered the ordination of the candidates whom Constantine and Methodius presented, and authorized the use of the Slavic liturgy. Constantine survived his triumph but a few months. Broken in health, he retired to an Italian monastery where he assumed the name of Cyril and died on February 4, 869.

Meanwhile, in Pannonia, Prince Kotzel became worried over the long absence of the young priests he had detailed for ordination. When he sent a special mission to inquire about them, the Pope dismissed Methodius and his followers with a letter addressed jointly to Rostislav, to the latter's nephew Svatopluk, and to Kotzel, stating that he was designating Methodius as an emissary not merely to Pannonia, but to Moravia as well, but, fearful of irritating the Frankish clergy, he momentarily abstained from naming Methodius Bishop of Pannonia, as Kotzel preferred, since this action would have detached Pannonia from the diocese of Salzburg. His hesitation was banished, however, by Rostislav's military successes against Louis the German in 869, which diminished the authority of the Frankish clergy, and also by the news that Boris of Bulgaria was turning from Rome to Byzantium. In order to block any further expansion of Byzantine influence and to tie the Danubian Slavs more closely to Rome, he thus consecrated Methodius as Archbishop of Pannonia and named him papal legate to all the Slavs.

The success of this design was almost immediately compromised by unforeseen political developments. In 870, Rostislav was deposed by his nephew Svatopluk, who became a Frankish vassal. On his arrival in Moravia, Methodius was arrested and brought before a court comprising the bishops of Passau, Salzburg, and Freising, who professed total ignorance of his new episcopal status. Far from doing anything to protect Methodius, Svatopluk was actually present when Hermanarich, Bishop of Passau, struck the Greek bishop with his whip. Discovering, however, that he was merely the catspaw of the Franks, Svatopluk soon reversed his field and by 874 was independent. The curia meanwhile endeavored to ascertain what had happened to Methodius. The Bishop of Freising denied to

Conversion and Religious Divisions 61

Pope Adrian that he even knew him, but after Adrian's death in 872, his successor John VIII sent a special legate to Louis the German with orders suspending two of the offending bishops and directing the primate of Salzburg to release Methodius and to install him in his proper diocese. Unfortunately, however, John was obliged to placate the Germans, and compromised to the extent of forbidding Methodius the use of the Slavic liturgy, though he permitted preaching in the vernacular.

Since 867 events had moved rapidly in Constantinople itself. Basil I, the bold and able successor of Michael III, whom he had murdered, revived the Byzantine navy, drove the Arabs from the Adriatic, and gradually reëstablished Greek ascendancy over the Croat tribes of the shoreline, who maintained their independence from the Frankish yoke that weighed upon their inland kindred, and therefore for the moment gravitated toward Byzantium. Basil thus secured not only the submission of the Serbs and the coastal tribes as far as Dalmatia, but also sent missionaries to baptize any remaining pagans. Dalmatia was then subjected in 878, and more missionaries accompanied the new Greek administration. Since the Bulgarians had been affiliated with Constantinople since 870, this date represents the high watermark of Byzantine influence in the Balkans. In 879, however, the Grecophile Croat princes were opposed by a revolt which brought the Dalmatian coastal area once more into the Roman sphere. This development defined the future limits of Byzantine influence. It remained dominant in Serbia and on the Croat coast as far as Dalmatia, as well as among the Slavs in Bulgaria, Thrace, and the Greek peninsula.

In connection with the Serbs, we should note here that the faith reached them from two directions. The territory south of Pannonia and west of the Balkan Morava River, which joins the Danube east of Belgrade, was evangelized by Roman priests from the coast as early as the eighth century. On the other hand, the conversion of the Slavs in western Macedonia, whether Bulgarians or Serbs, proceeded from Salonika at approximately the same time, but was most intense during the reign of Basil I.

Methodius had not obeyed the Pope's injunction to abandon the Slavic liturgy but, when summoned to Rome in 879 to explain his position, was again victorious on even this point. John VIII, however, endeavored to conciliate Svatopluk, who had never been personally sympathetic toward Methodius, by naming as the latter's suffragan the Prince's favorite priest, one Wiching, who immediately took the side of the Frankish clergy and blocked Methodius at every turn. The Archbishop eventually decided to shift his activities further south, and in 881 set forth on a journey toward the valleys of the Drave and the Save, where he received an invitation from Basil I to visit Constantinople. The Patriarch Photius was, after all, an old friend, and the Emperor himself was well-informed of Methodius's activities in a frontier area not entirely alien to Greek interests.

Upon his return to his diocese Methodius at first concentrated his efforts on translating additional canonical books and ecclesiastical texts. Unfortunately for his pastoral work, however, John VIII was poisoned in 882, and under Stephen V hostile exchanges between Rome and Byzantium were resumed. Methodius himself died in April, 885, after designating as his successor Gorazd, his most capable disciple. Wiching, Methodius's old enemy, straightway renewed his intrigues and had no trouble in securing the favorable ear of a pope already irritated against Byzantium. Stephen V abandoned the Slavic liturgy altogether, Wiching's partisans secured the eternal exile of Gorazd and the other disciples of Methodius, and thus the work of twenty years in Moravia was wiped out.

After the decision of Prince Boris of Bulgaria to accept conversion in 862, the next twenty years were marked by fruitless papal attempts to gain control of the Bulgarian church. In 870, indeed, the Eighth Oecumenical Council, under the influence of Basil I, had formally decided that the Bulgarian church was subject to the patriarchate of Constantinople, and

Roman priests were thereafter excluded from the country. The archbishop of Bulgaria ranked next after the patriarch so that his diocese was practically autonomous, and Boris had good reason to resist all further Roman overtures and blandishments. Greek influence was therefore greatly intensified in Bulgaria, though the Byzantines were tactfully careful not to use their missionary activities for political ends. Besides Methodius, during his visit to Constantinople in 881, had given brilliant accounts of the results of his Moravian efforts in the vernacular. These reports aroused in both Basil I and Photius the idea that they could advance the good cause in Bulgaria by similar means, and a training school for Slavic priests was opened on the Bosporus.

After the elimination of Methodius's disciples from Moravia in 885, some of them were sold into slavery and were accidentally discovered by a Greek envoy in the slave market at Venice. They were immediately redeemed by the Byzantine envoy and taken to Constantinople where Basil hastened to assign them to Bulgarian charges. At the same time Clement and the other disciples of Methodius who had been put across the Danube arrived at the Bulgarian frontier fortress of Belgrade, whence they were sent on to Boris's court at Pliska, where they were cordially welcomed. At the moment the Greek court favored Slavic priests, hence there could be no objection to their employment in Bulgaria, even if the local Greek clergy viewed them with a somewhat jaundiced eye.

Unfortunately, however, Basil I died in the summer of 886, and Photius, the great patriarch and the friend of Constantine and Methodius, was supplanted by an insignificant successor. Boris therefore decided not to provoke the influential Greek clergy needlessly. He kept them at his court, but sent Clement and his associates to work among the people in Macedonia, which he hoped might develop into a promising stronghold of purely Slavic Christianity.

Boris abdicated in 889, and during the next thirty years, under the rule of his son Simeon, Bulgaria, despite varying fortunes, not only threw off even the vestiges of a Byzantine protectorate but also extended its domain far into Serbia. During this interval Clement's activity greatly expanded. He founded the great monastery of Saint Panteleimon at Okhrida, and on Simeon's accession he was consecrated a bishop. The legacy of Constantine and Methodius was thus preserved in all its wealth, to the great advantage of Bulgaria, which thus became a purely Slavic country with an autonomous church. Simeon was accordingly able to realize his father's ambition of proclaiming a Bulgarian patriarchate.

Obviously the roots of the culture disseminated by the Bulgarian church, however nationalistic, were essentially Byzantine. Though a Slav by birth, Clement himself had been trained by Greek masters, and Simeon too was culturally so Hellenized as to be nicknamed the "half-Greek." Hence the literary productions of the Macedonian schools founded by Clement and his associates were, if not mere translations, usually slavish imitations of Greek texts. Simeon himself composed an anthology of texts compiled from Greek theologians. Though the influence of Byzantine letters during this epoch was limited to the theological and the liturgical sphere, it is of relatively enormous significance that at the end of the ninth century and the beginning of the tenth the Old Bulgarian language was being adopted for literary purposes under Greek influence, and that a large body of Slavic-speaking priests was being created who were capable of transmitting at least the ecclesiastical aspects of Greek culture in their own tongue. The mission of Constantine and Methodius thus bore fruit, not on the ground they themselves sowed, but on territory closer to Byzantium, so that the results of what their disciples accomplished in Bulgaria could be easily drawn upon seventy-five years later when a much more extensive field was opened with the conversion of the south Russian principality of Kiev.

At the same time, the Slavic liturgy which had been proscribed in Moravia was also transmitted through Pannonia into Croatia, but in general the popes saw no reason to use it

Conversion and Religious Divisions 65

as an instrument once Byzantine encroachments were no longer feared, especially since the local bishops were liable to Roman influence, and the Slavic princes themselves were anxious to placate the romance-speaking populations of the wealthy coastal cities. But with the exception of Croatia, the work of Constantine and Methodius brought all the South Slavs and later the Eastern Slavs under the cultural aegis of Byzantium.

The Slovenes, the Czechs, and the Moravians had fallen, as we have seen, to the lot of Rome. While the Slovenes, by withdrawing southward from the Danube, were able to escape total absorption by the Germans, their Slavic kindred on the Baltic coast and in the interior of Germany faced infinitely more critical circumstances. The Saxon clergy were eager for landed possessions, and the easiest way to obtain them was by evangelizing the Transelbian Slavs, whose conversion would also pour tithes into their coffers. German expansion at the expense of the Western Slavs was most drastically pursued during the reign of Otto I (936-973). Beyond the Elbe a swarm of bishoprics arose, half houses of God, half fortresses. The Slavs became tributary as far as the Oder. They retained their landed possessions, but all unoccupied land was transferred from the Slavic chiefs to the German crown. Royal vassals were placed in the tribal centers to operate the administration, and bishoprics were established along the eastern border. Forcible conversion of the Slavic natives became the order of the day. Narrow as their margin of living was, the Slavic peasants were driven to rigorous abstention from labor on the numerous saints' days. The spiritual content of their conversion was actually so slight at this period that it is actually recorded how the Slavic peasants who were laboriously taught to say *Kyrie eleison* in the right places sullenly parroted it with like-sounding Slavic words which mean "in a crooked alder-bush." Indeed, the avarice and oppression of both clergy and nobles provoked violent outbreaks of resentment among the Transelbian Slavs in 982, 1018, and 1066, which cost many German lives and threw the colonizers back across the Elbe, so that it was not until the middle of the twelfth century that German domination was reëstablished between the Elbe and the Oder.

The beginnings of the Polish state fall, as it happens, within the period characterized by German pressure on the Baltic Slavs during the reign of Otto I. About 963 the pagan Polish prince Mieszko I ruled over a realm east of the Oder and south of Pomerania and modern East Prussia, which included the middle and upper Vistula basin, stretching further southward to the Czech border at the Sudetens, and comprising most of Volhynia. The German Margrave Gero, whose territory included a good part of modern Saxony, subjugated the Slavic Lusatians (Liticians) and Milchanians of the upper Spree valley. These tribes extended eastward to the Oder and the Bober, and were thus in close contact with the western Polish peoples. At the same time, German penetration threatened Silesia southwest of the upper Oder, and in 979 the Margrave Odo even endeavored to force Mieszko to pay tribute on the area between the Oder and the War—the rivers (that is, roughly, between Frankfurt-Glogau and Posen). This expedition resulted in a German defeat, but the German menace had already induced Mieszko to improve his standing by affiliating himself with a Christian reigning family and to embrace the faith himself.

In spite of his previous record of polygamy, he married Dubravka (Bona), sister of the Czech prince Boleslav I, in 966, and was converted. The Polish bishopric of Posen was founded in 968. It was subject to the archdiocese of Magdeburg, and its first encumbent was a German cleric. Mieszko then made his submission to Otto in Quedlinburg on Easter Day, 973. After Otto I's death, German relations with Poland were more or less in abeyance until 984. Meanwhile Dubravka had died in 977, whereupon Mieszko married Oda, previously a nun, the daughter of the Margrave Thiedrich. Mieszko himself died in 992 as a faithful vassal of Otto III. His son and successor, Boleslav the Brave, maintained the same policy with such success that he won the respect of both Otto III and Pope Sylvester II

(Gerbert d'Aurillac). Otto's temperament was singularly open to foreigners, and he conceived an intense regard for Boleslav which the latter was not beyond exploiting. Knowing that Otto's friend Adalbert, former Bishop of Prague, had been slain on a missionary journey to the Prussians in 999, Boleslav successfully endeavored to recover his relics. Otto was thus induced the next year to make a pilgrimage to Gnesen, where they were preserved. He relieved Boleslav of the previous tribute to the empire, made Gnesen an archbishopric, and transferred Posen to the archdiocese of Mainz. Polish bishoprics dependent on Gnesen were also set up in Breslau, Krakow, and Kolberg (Pomerania). Though he could not entirely throw off German vassalage, Boleslav thus made the Polish church practically independent of German influence.

During the ninth century ambitious Vikings from Sweden settled in the Slavic trading centers on the Russian water courses, established themselves as a ruling class, and organized two strong points at Novgorod and Kiev at either extremity of the great trade route from the Baltic to the Black Sea. Extending its authority over neighboring tribes and cities, Kiev in the tenth century became a rising principality largely supported by commerce. Its princes raided the shores of the Black Sea, and its commercial contacts with Byzantium were regulated by extant treaties as early as 907. One Kievan prince even ventured to attack Constantinople in 941. Another member of the ruling house, the Princess Olga (she was of pure Swedish blood), visited Constantinople and was converted in 957. Though there were some Christians in Kiev from that early date, her son Sviatoslav refused to change his faith. During his campaigns of 967-971 in Bulgaria, he seriously menaced the Greek capital. But his son Vladimir was destined to play an even more conspicuous role in Byzantine diplomatic and dynastic history.

Vladimir succeeded to the principate in 977. He had extensive Scandinavian connections, and was highly successful in subjecting Slavic tribes of the periphery. He was in close contact with the Poles, and among his concubines were several Christian girls of either Greek or Slavic blood. He was not without interest in religion as such, having staged a sort of pagan revival in Kiev at the opening of his reign. There is some likelihood that frequent exchanges with Byzantium had caused him to entertain the idea of conversion before 987, but in that year an unusual combination of circumstances pushed him toward a decision.

John Tzimisces, one of the greatest of Byzantine generals and victor over Vladimir's father Sviatoslav in Bulgaria, had died in 976 after reigning as emperor of Byzantium for six years. He was succeeded on the throne by two youthful sovereigns, Basil II and Constantine. Since their prestige was slight, their authority was almost immediately menaced by a military revolt, the leader of which even occupied Scutari, opposite Constantinople. As soon as the revolt broke out, Basil entered into correspondence with Vladimir in the hope of winning an alliance and auxiliary troops. Vladimir was disinclined to furnish this aid without commensurate reward, and coupled with his assent the condition that the emperors should give him their sister Anna in marriage. Up to this point Byzantine sovereigns had normally been chary of marrying their female relations to alien princes. Constantine Porphyrogenitus had laid down the principle twenty-five years before that no Byzantine princess should marry a foreign potentate unless he were baptized. The German emperor Otto I had vainly negotiated in behalf of his son for the hand of the emperors' sister whom Vladimir now sought. But the situation of the empire was too critical to brook long delay, and the emperors consented to the marriage provided Vladimir would accept conversion.

The Prince of Kiev then supplied six thousand troops who helped to repress the rebellion during the summer of 988. But once the fortunes of the emperors began to rise, they showed manifest reluctance to execute the part of the bargain which concerned the Princess Anna. Vladimir, for his part, had taken this stipulation very seriously and intended it should be enforced. So while his troops were still assisting the Byzantines during the summer of 989, he besieged and captured the Greek city of Chersonesus on the western Crimean coast about three miles south of modern Sevastopol, after which he sent envoys to Constantinople with the warning that if the princess were not sent to meet him he would attack the capital. Basil and Constantine were thus induced to carry out their share of the contract, and Anna departed tearfully with a numerous suite for Chersonesus, where Vladimir's baptism and his marriage were duly solemnized.

After restoring Chersonesus to the Greeks, Vladimir returned to Kiev accompanied by the priests in Anna's entourage, and there proceeded to convert his subjects with the same forthright energy he showed in other crises. He caused the local idols to be overthrown, and the local population was subjected to wholesale baptism in the Dnieper river which flows past the city. As conversion progressed, the principate was divided into eight eparchies, each under a bishop. During the next century, however, Christianity spread rather slowly, as is indicated by outbreaks of paganism fifty and even eighty years later under the leadership of local shamans.

The conversion of the masses was to some extent accelerated by a facile syncretism which assimilated the figures of Christian belief to the chief dieties of the rudimentary pagan Slavic cult. Perun the thunderer was identified with the prophet Elijah in his chariot of fire, and it was also an easy step from belief in Svarog, the god of fire, and in his son Dazhbog, the life-giving solar orb, to an elementary conception of Almighty God the Father and the Son, the light of the world and of truth. The pagan Slavs' conceptions of an omnipotent multitude of benign or hostile supernatural beings were satisfied by the Christian notions of the Virgin, of saints, and of devils. Conversion also provided the upper classes with a general basic philosophy or *Weltanschaung* and with abundant ritual answers to their common human speculations. It likewise endowed them with an ideal of conduct which, though hardly attained by every individual, nevertheless produced some admirable characters among early medieval churchmen and laymen.

The sources from which Vladimir drew his clergy present a problem of some importance and complexity. Adequate evidence exists that Greek priests were sent to Russia both in the suite of the Princess Anna and after her marriage to Vladimir. Since there were isolated Christians and at least one church at Kiev prior to Vladimir's conversion, there must have been a small nucleus of Russian-speaking clergy in the city itself before 989, though these clerics were probably of Greek nationality. Vladimir's well-attested activity in wholesale conversion even among the masses at widely separated points makes it likely, however, that some provision was made for evangelizing the people in a language comprehensible to them. Priests with the appropriate linguistic qualifications could be found at this period only among members of the Byzantine clergy who had been active in Bulgaria or among the Bulgarian clergy themselves, since the differentiation between the spoken languages of Bulgaria and south Russia in the late tenth century was so slight as to constitute no barrier to common understanding.

The tradition of vernacular religious culture under Greek intellectual auspices had been established in Bulgaria during the reigns of Boris (852-889) and Simeon (894-927). In the light of the eventual transmission to Kiev of a large body of ecclesiastical literature in Old Bulgarian translations, it is an accepted and doubtless correct convention of Russian literary history in the pre-Tartar period to assume that these works were first transmitted to Kievan Russia through the medium of Byzantium as priests were sent out into the Russian field. But, curiously enough, there are no historical data behind this respectable hypothesis, nor does any explicit evidence point to the slightest direct contact between the charges of Bulgaria and Russia during the principates of Vladimir and of his son through 1045.

While some ingenious theories to the contrary have been expounded, the fact remains that Byzantine relations with Bulgaria were constantly hostile from Vladimir's conversion to his death in 1015. Basil II would thus hardly have attached to an enemy state the young church founded by his brother-in-law. There is therefore no motive for believing that the Russian church at its foundation was other than an eparchy of the Byzantine patriarchate, even if we admit the contention that there was no metropolitanate in Russia during Vladimir's lifetime. In the transmission of Slavic liturgical and theological texts at this period the mediation of Constantinople was inevitable, and the priests at Vladimir's disposal must have likewise been chiefly Greeks, some of whom possessed a smattering of Bulgarian from work in Bulgaria itself or, like the protoapostles Constantine and Methodius, from their contacts in the northern and western marches of the Byzantine Empire.

That Vladimir assimilated certain intellectual interests along with the faith is indicated by his insistence upon some degree of education among the children of his followers. The *Primary Chronicle* reports:

He took the children of the best families and sent them for instruction in book learning. The mothers of these children wept bitterly over them, for they were not yet strong in faith, but mourned as for the dead.

It is not clear whether Vladimir intended that these youths should be trained as priests or as civil servants, but from the facts that within the next fifty years educated Russian priests come to the fore and that extensive reference is made in the sources to the culture of Vladimir's son and successor Yaroslav the Wise, it is fair to suppose that Vladimir had his eye on both professions. In Constantinople at the close of the tenth century interest in higher education was restricted by the general attention to military problems and conquest, so that book learning was primarily a matter of personal and private study. It is therefore unlikely that Vladimir had before him any models calculated to inspire the establishment of schools in the modern or even the medieval sense of the word, but rather that he employed the priests sent from Byzantium as private teachers for the younger members of prominent families connected with his court.

At any rate, extant literary monuments dating from the last half of the eleventh century give evidence of an expanding nucleus of culture in Kiev itself which is the direct result of Vladimir's concern for education. It was hardly to be expected that a tremendous outburst of literary energy would ensue as soon as the seeds of learning were sown among a younger generation sprung from illiterate Varangian and Slavic sires, but the readiness with which Byzantine hagiographical and annalistic models were assimilated and imitated even before 1100 indicates an extensive interest in reading among circles brought up in a tradition of culture to the founding of which Vladimir contributed. That the basis of this culture was mere literacy—the ability to read the Psalms, the Gospels, and such Byzantine religious or historical compilations as had been translated into old Bulgarian in the days of Boris and Simeon—by no means lessens the importance of Vladimir's zeal for intellectual progress.

To Vladimir also belongs the credit for initiating the construction program which within the next century transformed Kiev into one of the most impressive medieval cities. The crowning structural exploit of Vladimir's reign was thus a stone church of the Virgin, begun in 989, for the erection and decoration of which he imported artisans from Greece. It was completed and consecrated in 996. At its dedication Vladimir endowed it with a tithe of his property and income, from which donation is derived its customary name, The Church of the Tithe, or *Desiatinnaia*. Originally a basilica, it was reconstructed with five cupolas after a fire in 1017, and collapsed under the weight of a crowd of refugees when the Tartars took

Conversion and Religious Divisions 73

Kiev in 1240. No remnant of it now survives except the ruins of its foundations.

In Vladimir's day the clergy rapidly assumed a place among the ruling class. Apart from introducing new notions of judicial procedure derived from the Greek *Nomokanon,* the early clergy also undertook to advise Vladimir on affairs of state and local policy. In 992 the bishops advised the substitution of corporal punishment for fines in order to suppress brigandage and similarly suggested that the proceeds of fines in other cases should be spent on military equipment for defense against the menacing nomads. The ecclesiastical courts also assumed jurisdiction over numerous social problems and offenses which took new significance in the light of the Christian moral code: bigamy, divorce, heresy, sacrilege, witchcraft, and adultery. Vladimir thus tolerated the fusion of church and state on the basis of contemporary Byzantine usage.

By the process of conversion among the various Slavic groups, the bases of cultural and political differentiation were thus laid before the year 1000. Exposed to Christian influences since the seventh century, the Slovenes were converted by Bavarian clergy, and after their absorption into the Carolingian empire in 788, remained until the first World War in submission to one German state or another. The Croats, though in contact with the mission of Constantine and Methodius, reverted to Rome after the disciples of Methodius were expelled from Moravia, and have come down through the ages as Catholics, whatever their political allegiance. The Slavs along the Elbe and the Baltic were subjected to the most violent political and religious pressure from Saxon priests and nobles with the result that, despite heroic revolts, they were slowly pushed back toward the former Polish frontier. The Byzantine influence in Moravia lasted but a quarter of a century before the work of the proto-apostles, Constantine and Methodius collapsed, and the Moravians, like the Czechs, remained under the pastoral care of bishops of the Roman rite. Though the spirit of Bohemian individualism rose again during the Hussite Wars of the early fifteenth century, and was not extinguished even after the accession of the Hapsburgs in 1526, in our own time, after triumph and defeat, it will (we hope) rise to play a worthy role in a better world.

The Poles have never departed from the faith that Mieszko I brought them in 963, and their whole cultural evolution is intimately dependent upon the civilizing mission of the Roman Church; if ever their faith was firm, they need it doubly now. The Serbs and Bulgarians were ecclesiastically dependent from the ninth century on Byzantium, and we have seen how the intellectual nationalism of Boris and Simeon built up a treasury of native Slavic culture derived from Byzantine sources. Upon this treasury the Russian Church drew as soon as it was founded, and without Simeon's policy of ecclesiastical autonomy the rapid advance of medieval Russian culture would have been greatly retarded. After the fall of Byzantium before the Turks in 1453, Russia remained the sole great repository of Byzantine and Greek Orthodox religious tradition until thirty years ago.

IV

The Formation of Russia

We have already spoken of the contacts of the primitive Slavs with the Goths during the latters' migrations of the early Christian era and the succession of invasions from Asia into the steppe country which exerted political and some cultural influence upon the Eastern Slavic tribes. At the time of the conversion of the Russians in 989 during the reign of Vladimir I at Kiev, the principality of Kiev was already a state of growing area and rising influence. It is now relevant to discuss the process by which this principality was founded, and to carry the history of the Russian state five centuries beyond Vladimir to the domination of Moscow, showing the course of events by which the national nucleus was transferred from the Ukraine to the younger northeastern principality.

In Scandinavia, and particularly in Sweden, the period from 750 to 800 A.D. was marked by pronounced activity in organization and conquest. During the ninth century Swedish interest in oriental commerce developed rapidly and caused such an active search for lines of eastward communication that before 850 Swedish settlers appeared on the southeastern shore of Lake Ladoga. About the year 900, a Swedish colony was founded at Gnezdovo, near modern Smolensk, and Swedish immigration reached the headwaters of the rivers Volga and Oka. Finds of Swedish *objets d'art* of the ninth and tenth centuries along the northern Russian watercourses which provide an easy route between the Baltic and the Volga indicate a lively activity in oriental trade, and the Swedish colonies in this area result from the opening, by the Swedes, of a new trade route to the Orient via the Volga.

In 859, according to the Russian *Primary Chronicle*, "Varangians from beyond the sea" imposed tribute on the northernmost Slavs in Russia and their Finnish neighbors. Within the next four years, the tributaries revolted and expelled the invaders, but finding themselves unable to preserve order, they were obliged (according to the *Chronicle*) to invite the return of their oppressors. The story continues that in response to this plea, three Varangian brothers, Rurik, Sineus, and Truvor, migrated to Russia with their kin. Rurik settled in Novgorod, two of his retainers wrested Kiev from the Khazars, and Oleg, allegedly, the regent for Rurik's young son Ivor, took Kiev from them after Rurik's death. The legendary date of the traditional calling of the princes thus harmonizes with the archaeological evidence as to the period of Scandinavian immigration. Both the *Primary Chronicle* and Arabic geographical sources refer to these immigrant Scandinavians as Rus (Russes), a name which was later applied to the Slavs they subdued and to the state which grew from the principalities they created. The Volga trade route which they first discovered rapidly declined in importance once they found that the Dnieper offered relatively easy access to Byzantium.

The civilization which the immigrant Swedes brought with them to Russian territory was essentially that of the Viking Age. The Scandinavian artifacts of the ninth and tenth centuries discovered in Russian territory indicate that their makers and owners were possessed of no mean talent in working metals (bronze, silver, gold), and were found of tasteful adornment. From their northern homes they brought a highly developed capacity for handling iron tools. Not only had the Vikings in general mastered the technique of timbered houses, but they were also capable of constructing clinker-built sea vessels up to fifty feet in length and sturdy cargo boats of as much as fifty tons' burden, though for river navigation they used lighter craft. Where the aboriginal Slav of the Russian plains and forests was poor in weapons—even his word for sword (as we know) he had been forced to borrow from the invading Goths—the Swedish adventurer wielded a heavy, straight, two-edged blade and the battle-ax which later became the distinguishing weapon of the Byzantine emperors' Varangian guard.

In the main the Scandinavian immigrants to Russia from Sweden belonged to the yeoman class and apart from naval raids on the Black Sea coast generally abstained from the deeds of violence which characterized Viking visitations in Western Europe. The native Slavs were too humbly endowed to offer rich booty, and the Russes were manifestly more interested in setting up ordered and profitable commercial settlements than in the commission of futile barbarities other than those incidental to the habitual slave traffic. The tradition that Rurik and his brethren were accompanied by their kinsfolk would suggest that the social organization of the immigrant Swedes was still on the clan basis, and that the senior of the clan functioned as chieftain or *konungr,* supported by a *comitatus* (bodyguard, retinue) of his more or less distant relatives and accepted retainers. The Scandinavian energy and skill at arms, coupled with a pronounced gift for discipline and organization, stood the scattered Eastern Slavic tribes and embryonic towns in good stead at a moment when a cohesive impulse was essential for their survival.

Having settled along the Dnieper as far as Kiev, the Russes soon entered into commercial relations with the Khazar khanate, and after a raid on Constantinople in 860, regular commerce developed between the Greek empire and the cities on the Dnieper trade route. The chief Russian points of origin for this trade were Novgorod, Smolensk, Lubech, Chernigov, and Kiev. The Norse sources also mentioned Murom, Rostov, and Suzdal on the northeast, which owed their importance to the Volga artery. It is a historical fact of prime importance that the Scandinavian warrior-merchants who settled among the primitive Eastern Slavs founded no new towns themselves, but by their superior energy and military prowess made themselves the ruling class in urban centers of population which already existed. They were not the creators of the river-borne commerce from which they gained their livelihood. The routes and staples of this commerce had been defined far back in the early ages of the Mediterranean world, and the Russes who built up prosperous commercial relations with Byzantium simply renewed a system of exchange temporarily disjoined by the vicissitudes of nomadic movements.

Kiev was the chief trading post of the lower Dnieper valley, the center at which merchandise was collected for shipment to the Crimea or to Byzantium. The Viking or so-called Varangian chief who controlled Kiev was thus likely to surpass in wealth and prestige his competitors in the more northern cities. The domestic activity of a Kievan prince of the early tenth century consisted chiefly in collecting tribute in kind, the proceeds of which not only supported his family and the retainers on whom his military power was founded, but also served as a basis for trade, which was under the prince's direct control. As the early Varangian princes imposed their sovereignty over successive towns, they delegated a viceroy to each, but the practice of assigning junior princes of the ruling family to subject cities begins only with Prince Sviatoslav (956-972), father of Vladimir I, under whom the Russians were converted. By the early tenth century, the outlying tribes had been tied together in a loose confederation connected with Kiev by economic interests dictated by trade with Constantinople, and this trade was regulated by a formal treaty as early as 907.

The magnificence of the Byzantine capital early exercised its attraction on the Kievan aristocracy. Vladimir's grandmother, the Princess Olga (a lady of pure Scandinavian stock) not only administered the principality after her husband's violent death, but in 975 became a convert to Christianity and made a ceremonial visit to Constantinople, where she was sumptuously entertained by the Emperor Constantine Porphyrogenitus, who has left us a detailed account of the occasion. Her son Sviatoslav, Vladimir's father, remained a convinced pagan, and is best known to history for his overthrow of the Khazar khanate in 962, his extension of Kievan authority to the upper Volga, and his disastrous attempts to subjugate Bulgaria between 968 and 971. He was, in fact, slain by the nomad Pechenegs at the rapids of the Dnieper while returning home from a crushing defeat at the hands of the Byzantine emperor John Tzimisces.

After his father's death Vladimir, who at the time was prince of Novrogod, opened hostilities against his half-brother who had succeeded Sviatoslav, and by his opponent's death became heir to Kiev. Before his conversion he had consolidated his power in the Dnieper valley, confirmed his father's conquest of the region between the Dnieper and the upper Volga, pushed his domains to the northeastern river courses feeding the Baltic, and made important gains at the expense of the Poles in Volhynia and Galicia. His ingenuity transformed a loose confederation with but weak control of its periphery into a unified Russian domain. That this unity was maintained with difficulty under his immediate descendants and was eventually dissolved was a consequence of local particularism aggravated by economic derangement, of feuds in the princely family, and of the pressure of nomad invaders.

The principality of Kiev became a state of European importance by Vladimir's conquests and conversion. The reign of his son Yaroslav the Wise from 1017 to 1054 is the meridian of its greatness. Yaroslav himself was a prince of rare intelligence and broad international contacts. He had himself married Ingigerd, a Swedish princess who had earlier been engaged to King Olaf Haraldsson of Norway. His sister Maria married King Kizimir I of Poland; of his daughters, one married King Henry I of France; a second Harald the Severe, King of Norway; a third King Andrew of Hungary. His son Vsevolod was the husband of a Greek princess, and the son of this union eventually became the consort of Gytha, daughter of the Saxon Harold who fell at Hastings in 1066. Kiev was thus united with contemporary European states by a series of dynastic alliances foreshadowing the customs of modern times.

Yet for all his power and wealth, Yaroslav governed by the same simple mechanism that had prevailed under Vladimir. The prince won his position by force and maintained it by personal supremacy, supported by Varangian mercenaries recruited from Scandinavia whenever domestic levies proved insufficient or disloyal, and consulting with his chief military aides, with the city elders, or with church dignitaries on matters of general policy. Yaroslav began the codification of customary civil and ecclesiastical law, encouraged both translations and original literature, and endeavored without success to emancipate the Russian Church from the Byzantine patriarchate. By his crushing victory over the nomad Pechenegs before the walls of Kiev in 1036, he made the marches of his principality safe for thirty-five years.

Beside rebuilding his father's Church of the Tithe after it was damaged by fire in 1017, he carried out a large-scale construction program which made Kiev one of the most notable medieval cities. His great cathedral of Saint Sophia in Kiev, with its five apses and thirteen cupolas, still contains the largest extant yardage of eleventh-century Byzantine frescoes and a series of remarkably preserved mosaics of impressive beauty. This is the one medieval Russian church which has been exhaustively studied by American archaeologists in coöperation with native Russian colleagues.

The underlying weakness of the Kievan principality lay in the fact that its stability was assured only by the prestige and ability of the ruling prince. There was as yet no sentiment of solidarity, national unity, and group interest which guaranteed that the whole system would not be overthrown by some ambitious and resolute rival from among the kindred princes in outlying cities loosely subject to the authority of the prince of

Kiev and envious of his power and wealth. Yaroslav himself was unable to obviate this danger. Before his death he endeavored to perpetuate the system his father and he had created by assigning the succession at Kiev to his eldest surviving son, and by apportioning to his younger sons the other important cities in the order of seniority of the princes and of the relative prestige of their several districts, with the recommendation that the younger brothers should regard the eldest as their sovereign and as the arbitrator of eventual disputes. Yet he omitted from his assignment his grandson and the descendants of his deceased brother, who thereupon constituted a potential threat to the tenure of the ruling line, even if the latter managed to keep peace among themselves.

The mode of succession established by Yaroslav thus placed the principality in the hands of a fraternal partnership. The apportionment of domains on the basis of seniority was theoretically feasible, however, only as long as the ruling family was small. But with the normal increase of direct and collateral descendants, mutual jealousies were bound to produce internal strife and to enfeeble the whole structure of the state. Mere seniority was no proof of either innate capacity or of the energy and tact required to allay disputes or to pacify ambitious rivals, and any weakness of the central authority impeded effective resistance to nomad attacks on the southern frontier. These attacks demanded at all times a vigorous defense, since cutting the Dnieper trade route meant decline of trade with Byzantium and interruption of the economic exchanges on which the prosperity of the principality depended. As it turned out, Prince Iziaslav, Yaroslav's son and successor, was unable to keep his rivals in check or even to maintain discipline among the unruly population of his capital. The Pechenegs, abolished as a menace by Yaroslav, were succeeded from 1062 by the nomad Polovtsi, whose boldness depended on what resistance they encountered. The disorders of Iziaslav's principate thus foreshadow a centrifugal movement destined to grow in volume until the preponderance of Kiev was utterly lost.

This process was occasionally delayed, if not arrested, by the appearance of competent princes who reëstablished for brief periods the stability and prestige of Kievan authority. For example, Vladimir Monomakh (1113-1125), grandson of Yaroslav, fought during his entire adult life either against the nomad Polovtsi or to maintain the unity of the principality against his kinsfolk, but such formal agreements as were reached for the assignment of domains to the various princely families were seldom of long standing. At the same time, the minor principalities of the western border were exposed to Polish or Hungarian aggression, and many southern frontier towns in the steppe country were either wiped out by the Polovtsi or abandoned because they might be.

The confusion which prevailed during the sixty years after Yaroslav's death in 1054 marks the onset of the decline of Kiev. While the feuds and disputes among the kindred princes were fought out by the princes themselves and their servitors, the lower classes of the population—the free peasants and the humble urban artisans—saw their fields laid waste and their earning power curtailed. If one prince occupied by force the domain of another and then was forced to withdraw, he frequently dragged off with him on his retirement the peasantry of the area he had temporarily occupied, and turned them into slaves in his own district. The result was a decrease in the free population and an enormous increase in the number of slaves available for work on princely estates.

By the end of the reign of Yaroslav the steppe country for one hundred miles or more south of Kiev had been settled by an agricultural population composed partly of free farmers, partly of war captives whom Yaroslav had located there, and partly by semicivilized pagans who had given up their nomad existence to live peacefully among their former foes and to form a sort of border militia. It was on this frontier population that the raids of the Polovtsi fell most heavily. The resulting migration from these exposed positions was most marked after 1125, but it began almost half a century earlier, and is reflected in the increased importance of the more remote northeastern domains of Rostov, Suzdal, and Murom, between the Oka and the Volga where the nomad menace did not reach.

While the inarticulate masses bore the brunt of the crisis, the wealth of the ruling class was for the moment not impaired, but rather enhanced. As long as the princes and their retainers were prosperous, the wealth of the Church also increased by grants and gifts. Monasteries multiplied and new churches were erected. Contact with Byzantium was still preserved. Through the expansion of the hierarchy under Greek guidance and example, the intellectual progress initiated by Yaroslav was intensified. To be sure, this culture remained aristocratic and ecclesiastical, but in this respect it hardly differed from the contemporary civilization of Western Europe, even though deprived of the continuity of classical tradition which lay at the root of the culture developed under the aegis of Rome. Marital alliances with German, Hungarian, and Polish princely families show at the same time that the Russian princes attached but slight importance to differences between the Eastern and Western Churches even after the schism of 1054.

No sooner had Vladimir Monomach died in 1125 when strife among the princes became rife once more. Competition for the control of Novgorod developed between the prince of Kiev and Monomach's son George whose domain lay at Suzdal in the northeast. Rival princes sacked and plundered one another's domains. One unpopular prince was even lynched by the angry Kievan populace. In 1149, Prince George captured Kiev himself, thus proving the vitality and resources of the northeastern area, but was unable to hold the metropolis permanently before 1155. When George died in 1160, however, the city had been fought over so constantly in the previous thirty years that practically all its dependent territory had been nipped off by neighboring principalities and it had been stripped of every element of its political prestige. Hence the possession of Kiev no longer conferred upon the ruling prince the slightest claim of primacy. Indeed, George's able son Andrew entertained no respect for Kiev at all and concentrated his efforts on enriching and adorning his own northeastern domain, which he ruled so autocratically that he was assassinated in 1174. Andrew's son Vsevolod who possessed equal capacity and better judgment, was recognized as a leader by all adjacent local princes, though he interfered but little in Kievan affairs and on the western Russian frontier the prestige of Vsevolod's domain was balanced by the rise of a powerful Galician principality. Kiev itself was disastrously sacked by the Polovtsi in 1203, and of this event a chronicler wrote, "No such woe had ever befallen Kiev during the whole time since conversion."

Amid the uncertainties of Russian political life at the beginning of the thirteenth century, the shadows of future events were already gathering. The German knights were moving up the Baltic coast, where Riga was founded in 1201. Their intrusion impelled the threatened Lithuanian tribes to unity, with the result that a Lithuanian state arose which began to absorb the northwestern Russian cities, though Russian culture in turn absorbed the conquerors. The Russians were not friendly to the Latin Empire of Byzantium after 1204, and it was in 1206 that the Mongols under Temuchin (better known as Genghis Khan) began their military expansion. But the Russian princes continued their petty quarrels, not suspecting the catastrophe that was impending.

The Mongols or Tartars first reconnoitered the country west of the Caspian in 1220, and the next year they menaced the Crimea and the steppe country, thus forcing the Polovtsi to apply for support to the Russian princes against whom they had so often fought. Since 1212, Kiev had been in the possession of Prince Mstislav, a member of the ruling family of Smolensk, able, courageous, and erratic; his wife was the daughter of a Polovtsian khan. The princes of Kiev, Chernigov, and Volhynia thus united with the Polovtsi against the Tartars, whom they met on the river Kalka, in the steppes near the

The Formation of Russia

Sea of Azov, in May 1224. Though the Russians were defeated and Mstislav of Kiev with other princes was slain, the Mongols contented themselves with pursuing the fleeing remnants of the Russian force to the Dnieper and then retired to Asia. Since the casualties at the Kalka entailed several dynastic changes, the domains of Chernigov, Kiev, and Galicia were now drawn into a loose confederation, while Suzdal controlled Novgorod, which opposed the Teutonic order and subjected the Finns of Esthonia and Karelia.

Meanwhile Genghis Khan had died in 1227, and eight years later his son and successor decided to renew the campaign into Europe under the command of Genghis Khan's grandson Batu. In 1237, after subjugating the Volga Bulgars near Kazan, Batu crossed the Volga to capture and sack the city of Ryazan, about one hundred miles southeast of Moscow. During the winter of 1237-38, the Mongols turned northward and burned the city of Vladimir, east of Moscow, after a successful siege. When Prince George II of Suzdal, whose family had perished, attacked the Tartars, he was defeated and killed. The invaders next started for Novgorod, but suspended the campaign because of the spring thaw, and went into summer quarters in the south near the mouth of the Don. Chernigov fell in 1239. The following autumn the Mongols appeared before Kiev and, as the *Chronicle* says,

> The Tartars took Kiev, and sacked St. Sophia and all the monasteries. And they took the icons, the holy crosses, and all church ornaments. But all the people, from small to large, they slew by the sword. This woe occurred before Christmas, on St. Nicholas' day.

By the fall of 1241, the Tartars had defeated the Poles at Liegnitz, crushed the Hungarians, and appeared before Vienna. But the fortunes of Europe changed, for Ugedei, the Great Khan, died, and Batu retired east to await the election of his successor. Yet he maintained his hegemony over Russia and set up his capital at Sarai on the lower Volga, just below Stalingrad, to which for two centuries the Russian princes, who were the vassals of Tartars, traveled to make submission.

The Tartar invasion aggravated the depopulation of the Kiev area which had begun under the Polovtsian menace. About the year 1300, even the metropolitan bishop of Kiev moved to Vladimir on the Klyazma, east of Moscow, and the remaining population took to the forests and hills. The result was a concentration of new settlements in the area immediately south of Moscow and considerable additions to the population of the western principality of Galicia-Volhynia, which became known as Little Russia, as opposed to Great Russia of the northeast. At the same time the northwestern principalities fell more and more into the hands of the rising Lithuanian state. The Galician-Volhynian principate was in a fair way to becoming an important national unit when it was devastated in 1283 by a Tartar expedition into Poland, with the result that Volhynia was taken over by the Lithuanians and Galicia by the Poles, who have held it intermittently from 1349 to the beginning of the second World War.

The economic results of the Tartar invasions were drastic even in the northeast. What national wealth was not destroyed by their pillage was extracted piecemeal by the process of collecting tribute. A population which had previously lived by hunting and fishing, importing its grain from the more fertile south, was now obliged to practice agriculture on comparatively unfavorable soil. A small amount of outside trade in furs, honey, and wax was maintained in order to secure silver with which to pay taxes, but domestic commerce was paralyzed and did not recover till the fifteenth century. Furthermore, even prior to the Tartar conquest, the Russian princes, despite their mobility, had begun to acquire fixed estates and thus to become landed proprietors. This process was accelerated by the Tartar hegemony since, for one thing, it was easier to collect tribute from a prince who was fixed, and besides it was difficult to obtain grants of new domains from the Tartars if a prince lost or surrendered his previous holdings. Hence the princes came to set more store by personal estates, and since the Tartars in their own interest were unlikely to tolerate any large principalities, the resulting dismemberment of the major units produced a large number of smaller domains, or appanages, which passed on by inheritance, whether or not the holder might become prince of some other area by the tender mercies of the Tartars. At the same time, the Tartar invasions greatly increased the number of landless peasants—dispossessed or impoverished small farmers—who became tenant farmers for large landlords on a quitrent basis.

Under Tartar hegemony the princes of Vladimir maintained at least a nominal control over the neighboring principalities and were the spokesmen of the Russian princes before the Tartar khans. These functions were, at any rate, sufficiently important and lucrative to inspire some rivalry for the possession of the title. In 1367 Prince Dmitri Donskoi erected a stone kremlin, or citadel, at Moscow and endeavored to subject the neighboring princes to his will. He met with some resistance from Prince Michael of Tver, who tried to purchase Tartar approval for himself, but was later forced to become Dmitri's vassal. The conditions of vassalage were such that dependent princes were obliged to supply Dmitri, as their overlord, with military aid, and when Dmitri won his famous victory over the Tartars in 1380 (the first case of successful Russian resistance), they supported him in this way.

The decline of the Tartars, manifested by conflicts of authority in the khanate itself, had begun almost a century before, and even prior to the year 1300 there were moments when the existence of two competing khans placed the Russian princes in a quandary. The struggle for supremacy between the princes of Tver and Moscow (which first became critical shortly before the year 1300) for supremacy as holders of the title Prince of Vladimir was also fought out in this interval. The dominance of Moscow was recognized in 1327 when Prince Ivan I secured authority to farm the Tartar taxes and began to increase his patrimony toward the north and east. The leadership of Moscow was further enhanced by the fact that the metropolitan of the Russian church moved over from Vladimir and took up his residence there. The rivalry of Tver was diminished and the chief competing power on Russian territory was Lithuania, which controlled most of White Russia and the northwest corner of the Ukraine.

Both the rise of Moscow and the further expansion of Lithuania were encouraged by dissensions which broke out among the Tartars in 1359 and considerably accelerated their decline. Olgerd, the reigning prince of Lithuania, captured Kiev in 1363 and advanced to the Black Sea. He then supported Tver against Moscow and in 1368 was barely prevented from taking the latter city by the new stone battlements which had just been constructed. He was then diverted from his central Russian operations by a war with Poland which cost him western Volhynia; his death in 1377 relieved Moscow for the moment of any Western threat. The Muscovites had no intention of handing back to the Tartars any privileges they had won while the latter were weak, and they were ready to fight for their retention. Such was the motive behind the provocative tactics by which Dmitri Donskoi jockeyed the Tartar Khan Mamai into a punitive expedition which the Russian prince defeated at great cost at Kulikovo Polye (Snipe Field) on the upper Don in 1380. However excessive the loss of life in this operation, the prince of Moscow became through this spectacular exploit the recognized national leader and his city the nucleus of patriotic sentiment. Unfortunately, the effort was so great that two years later the Tartars had no difficulty in entering and sacking the city of Moscow while Dmitri was absent. These events aroused once more the ambitious princes of Tver, whose influence Dmitri was able to cancel only by resuming a loyal feudatory relationship with the Tartars. It is significant nevertheless that Dmitri, on his death in 1389, bequeathed Vladimir to his son Basil I, though Basil was still

The Formation of Russia

obliged to secure Tartar ratification of his succession.

Events on the western front had meanwhile not stood still. Upon the death of King Kazimir the Great of Poland in 1370, his throne passed to his nephew, King Louis of Hungary. Louis in turn died in 1382 without male issue, so that the Polish crown devolved upon his thirteen-year-old daughter Yadwiga. Plans were then made to marry her to Prince Yagailo of Lithuania who had succeeded his father Olgerd in 1377. Upon becoming king of Poland in 1386, Yagailo made his cousin Vitovt prince of Lithuania. In this capacity Vitovt maintained friendly relations with the Tartar Khan Tokhtamysh, and he also married his daughter to Prince Basil I of Moscow. But when Tokhtamysh was deposed and fled to Vitovt's court, the latter's refusal to extradite him to his successor resulted in a collision with the Tartars in which Vitovt was soundly beaten. This defeat very largely eliminated the Lithuanian menace, and the consolidation policy of Moscow thus gained greater chances of success. It was momentarily checked in 1408, however, by a Tartar raid to the very gates of the city.

After the famous battle of Grünwald-Tannenberg in 1410, when the Polish-Lithuanian forces defeated the Teutonic knights, Vitovt's stock rose once more to the point where he was practically autonomous as the ruler of a principate which stretched from Memel and Smolensk to the Black Sea. Until his death in 1430 he never abandoned the hope of mastering Moscow, which at this period controlled an area barely one-third as large as his own. But his successor Svidrigailo became involved in a quarrel with Poland which prevented him from exerting any serious pressure on Moscow during the minority of Prince Basil II from 1425 on. Basil was also favored by the fact that many Tartar princes quit the disintegrating khanate and took service with Moscow, while others merely made themselves independent and under the name of Kazaks settled various localities in the Russian steppes. These independent Tartars are, then, the first Cossacks.

Basil II was to encounter, however, not only defeat and imprisonment at the hands of the Tartars but also the cruelty of a usurper who had him blinded. Luckily, however, the usurper's support was weak, and with aid from Tver Basil was restored. In 1452 he founded the Tartar principality of Kasimov under a friendly Tartar prince on the upper Oka east of Ryazan as a buffer against the hostile Tartars of Kazan, but now that not only Kazan but also the Crimea had split off from the old khanate, the latter was no longer a political threat of any consequence, and Basil II thus became the first prince of Moscow to emancipate himself completely from Tartar vassalage. Almost at the moment that Moscow became free Constantinople fell before the Turks, and the prince of Moscow became at one stroke the chief defender of the Orthodox faith and residuary legatee of the Byzantine tradition. Basil II was also successful in strengthening Muscovite influence in Novgorod, which had hitherto been prone to intrigue with Lithuania.

The expansion of Muscovite prestige undertaken amid such great difficulties by Basil II gathered new impetus during the reign of his son, Ivan III, who inherited the principality of Moscow in 1462. After first checkmating the Tartars by diplomatic agreements with adjacent oriental states, he attached himself to the Byzantine dynastic tradition by choosing, as his second wife, Zoe (Sophia) Palaeologa who, though stout and unattractive, was the niece of the last emperor of Byzantium. The Pope hoped this marriage might advance the union of the Eastern and the Western Churches, since Zoe had been raised a Catholic as his ward, and when she went to Moscow to be married in 1472, a papal legate accompanied her. He made no progress in his attempts to initiate negotiations, and Zoe's arrival was far more fruitful through the activities of the Italian architects and artisans whom she brought with her and who were soon adorning the Kremlin with Italianate churches and palaces. Ivan's designs against the Tartar khanate in the south were crossed by the Turks, who in 1475 subjugated both the khanate and the Crimea, and remained in southern Russia

The Formation of Russia

until the reign of Catherine II. At Novgorod, the pro-Lithuanian faction was still active despite the pledges exacted by Basil II. In 1475 Ivan personally visited the northern republic and three years thereafter the great commercial metropolis, long the only stronghold of democracy in Russia, was incorporated into the principality of Moscow. Thirteen years later the Tartar khanate of Kazan as a result of local dynastic rivalries also became a vassal, and an expedition in 1481 broke up the last vestiges of Tartar power on the Volga, where only Astrakhan remained in Tartar hands.

Ivan's reputation soon spread to western Europe, with the result that Emperor Maximilian I in 1488 sent an envoy to Moscow offering the prince a royal crown. Ivan was not unwilling to make a treaty with Maximilian covering mutual aid in case of a war with Poland, but remarked he did not need German confirmation of his royal status. On the Lithuanian side Ivan was equally fortunate since he forced the Lithuanians to abandon all claims on eastern Russian cities and to recognize him as "sovereign of all Russia" (*gosudar vseya Rusi*), while his daughter became the wife of the Prince of Lithuania. Under Ivan's son Basil III, who came to the throne in 1505, Pskov and Ryazan were added to the Muscovite domain, but relations with the Tartars both at Kazan and in the south were so far impaired that constant defensive measures were necessary on the southern frontier along the Oka.

When Basil died in 1533, his son Ivan IV (later known as the Terrible) was but three years old. The regency thus devolved till 1538 on the lad's mother, and from that date to 1547, when Ivan was crowned as tsar, upon a council of nobles in which factional politics were rife. It was from his experiences during this period that Ivan derived his intense hatred of the older feudal nobility as a class. Ivan finally conquered Kazan and annexed Astrakhan, thus placing the whole course of the Volga under Muscovite control. From that moment begins the Russian expansion into Siberia and the initiation of diplomatic relations with Khiva and Bokhara. At the same time the English, through Chancellor's expedition to the White Sea in 1553, opened up the northern sea route. Ivan was also conscious of the economic advantages of owning a Baltic port and began operations against the Livonian order of German knights which controlled both the Gulf of Riga and the Gulf of Finland. After capturing Narva, he founded the Russian navy a century and a quarter before Peter the Great by confiscating and arming a number of German merchant vessels, for which he employed German and Swedish officers as commanders. Ivan's early successes proved a boomerang, however, since the Livonian order was dissolved and Esthonia was turned over to Sweden. This event automatically produced a collision with that country, allied with Lithuania, so that war became incessant on the western front until Ivan's death in 1584.

By that date the formation and the future policy of modern Russia was clearly defined. It was a foregone conclusion that future Russian sovereigns would extend Russian territory to the Black Sea. It was only a question of time when the weakening of Poland and Lithuania would bring the Dnieper valley and White Russia under Muscovite sway. It had become a cardinal item of Russian policy to control the Finnish Gulf, and maritime commerce with the west would traverse those waters as soon as ports were either conquered or developed. The long period of Russian isolation from Europe was ended, and the difficult process of acquiring modern European techniques was about to begin. Russia had graduated from oriental domination and was on its way to becoming a major European power, never to approach the East again, save in the hope of conquest.

In view of the gradual evolution of Muscovite sovereignty, it is important to understand also the origins of autocracy in Moscow itself. For autocracy was by no means inevitable or universal in medieval Russia, and in the principality of Kiev the early princes had always had to reckon with town assemblies which supervised and even frequently deposed them. The influence of these assemblies was large in any medieval Russian city of which the economic and political status had been deter-

The Formation of Russia 93

mined independently of the princes, for one can appreciate that normal life went on even when princes shifted through inheritance or dynastic quarrels.

As a matter of fact in Novgorod, which was comparatively remote from either Kiev or Vladimir-Suzdal, the resident princes were merely delegates of the dominant state which momentarily enjoyed the lordship over the northern metropolis, but these resident princes changed so often that the citizens began to choose elective burgomasters early in the twelfth century. Eventually the princes surrendered even their control of the local courts, and in the course of time the whole administration of Novgorod and the areas it controlled became elective. The resident prince was thus transformed into a mere figurehead whose chief duty was to lead the military forces of this city-state. Popular sovereignty was expressed in the city assembly made up of all free citizens of whatever rank, and since this body was able to signify its will only by acclamation and sometimes even by pitched battles, the executive functions were exercised by a council composed of the bishop and various high elected officials, whether active or retired. The outlying domains of Novgorod—for eventually the republic colonized the territory as far as the White Sea and the Kola peninsula—enjoyed a considerable degree of autonomy, but always under the surveillance of a viceroy from the metropolis, though there are cases where citizens of these colonies participated in the city assembly at Novgorod itself. Pskov began its historical career as a dependency of Novgorod, but established its independence in 1347, when the men of Novgorod bound themselves by treaty not to send any viceroy to Pskov or to exercise any further judicial rights there.

The republican principle thrived in Novgorod and Pskov because actually the princes had contributed nothing to the civic and economic growth of these areas, which owed their expansion purely to the energy of their own citizens. But in northeastern Russia the situation was quite different. There, of the two dominant forces in contemporary society (the city assembly and the prince) only the prince remained, and became a landed proprietor who organized the economic activity of his subjects. If he shared his authority at all, it was not with the community but with other landed proprietors and with organs of the church to which he resigned judicial rights and the collection of dues. As early as the second half of the twelfth century, when immigration from the Kiev area to the northeastern principalities assumed large dimensions, Vladimir Monomach's grandson Prince Andrew already ruled as an autocrat in the domain of Suzdal and refused to recognize the rights either of nobles or of commoners as expressed in the town assemblies. This policy cost him his life, but after his assassination the older towns in this area were unable to maintain the principles of urban democracy even before the Tartar conquest wiped out this ideal. These towns were few in number, and the rural settlements were too scattered to acquire political cohesion. Later the onslaught of the Tartars so much impoverished even such towns as then existed that their pauperized inhabitants were more concerned about their daily bread than about political rights. Furthermore, the choice and confirmation of princes depended for the time being on the caprices of the invaders, so that this function, which had formerly belonged in practice to the city assembly, died out altogether, and when the assemblies occasionally convened, it was generally with the intention of rioting and revolting against Tartar exactions. The prince, ruling on Tartar sufferance, thus became the sole remaining possessor of local authority.

As we have seen, not until the middle of the fifteenth century was it absolutely clear that the nucleus of statehood in eastern Russia was definitely located at Moscow. By that time, the regional princes were permanently attached to their several domains which they ruled as feudal lords, supported by the contributions paid by the subjects who worked their lands, and there was no difference between minor and major princes in their proprietary attitude toward their landed possessions. Since their interests were thus predominantly economic, these

The Formation of Russia

princes began to develop a new group of aids who administered these interests, and such aids (who were actually officials, not nobles concerned with warfare) evolved into a new form of prince's council, or *duma*. The larger domains were split up into districts around important towns, and the districts into minor administrative divisions, all handled by appointees of the prince. These officials were far less concerned with the maintenance of public order or of civil rights than with seeing that the prince received his due financial return from the subject population, although church properties were usually exempt from their attentions. It is thus an open question whether there was any public law whatever in the early Muscovite period. In any event, the system shows the characteristic features of medieval feudalism: the dismemberment of state authority and its fusion with land ownership.

The rise of Moscow naturally produced a slow recovery from this parcellation, as the minor regional princes either voluntarily or under pressure surrendered their domains to the more powerful center. Novgorod was annexed outright by Ivan III after conquest had seriously diminished its outlying possessions. But especially during the last half of the fourteenth century, the gravitation toward Moscow moved with ever-increasing speed. On the other hand, the early Muscovite princes handled their new acquisitions purely as personal property. They bequeathed sections of it to their heirs, although soon it was the recognized practice to bequeath the lion's share to the oldest son. The logical conclusion from this tendency was first drawn by Ivan III after witnessing as a youth the vicissitudes of his father Basil II, who had almost lost the Muscovite domain because of feudal rivalries. Ivan refused to dismember his domain even in the interest of members of his family. His title of Great Prince (or Grand Duke) of all Rus he interpreted not merely in an honorific but in a juridical sense, and made it clear that he considered the whole domain as his personal patrimony. In this attitude he was confirmed less by pure selfishness than by the realization that only a unified state could resist both the Tartars and Lithuania, though in his will he did not break entirely with tradition, but bequeathed to his eldest son two-thirds of his landed possessions. Even so, however, the remaining regional princes ceased to be a menace, and the fact that his younger son was bound to serve Basil III as his overlord made the latter "sovereign of all Rus" in fact as well as in name. Such few regional princes as still existed merely held estates with rights of judgment and tribute, and were factually subject to the prince of Moscow. The title of tsar was first used by Ivan III in 1484, and in 1502 his son, Basil II, added the title "autocrat" (*samoderzhets*).

Such is the political, economic, and ideological process by which the power of Kiev was dissipated and, despite the competition of Lithuania, what was once a mere hunting lodge of the princes of Suzdal and Vladimir became the nucleus around which the modern Russian state took shape. It would be idle to pretend that this ideal was not realized without abundant propaganda from the Orthodox clergy who, particularly after the fall of Constantinople, wished to see the Prince of Moscow the head of Orthodox Christianity and the heir of Rome. Under the pressure of this new tradition, Basil III in particular, as the son of a princess of Byzantium, adorned his court with new ceremonial and assumed the device of the doubleheaded eagle which had belonged to his Byzantine forebears.

Thus the personal rule which had its origins in the decline of republican usages in northeastern Russia both before and since the Tartar conquest evolved into an absolutism founded upon dynastic tradition and supported by a nationalistic legend propagated by the church. The Muscovite tsar was not only the owner of his domain; he was God's anointed whom his subjects could approach only with fear and awe. The tsar's will was the will of God. As the heir of the Byzantine emperors, he acquired new authority over the church as the defender of the Orthodox faith. He confirmed the appointment of metropolitans and archbishops, even sometimes naming them without calling church councils, and clerics referred their disputes to his arbitration. Hence the tsardom of Muscovy became the finest flower of caesaro-papism.

While the last remnants of the old feudal regime were not entirely wiped out until Ivan the Terrible waged a war of annihilation against the jealous survivors of the regional nobility who opposed his system, its basis was securely laid before he came to the throne, and we therefore need not concern ourselves for the moment with his neurotic eccentricities or his administrative innovations.

V

Foundations of Russian Culture

Russia makes a relatively late appearance on the stage of European civilization. A specifically Russian culture does not even begin until nearly 1000 A.D. with the conversion of Prince Vladimir I of Kiev in 989. In Western Europe, since the fall of the Roman Empire, a new civilization had by that time evolved from a fusion of Christian ideals with the survivals of classical culture. But medieval Russia derived its faith from Byzantium and from the Eastern branch of the church in which purely Latin culture played a subordinate role, since the dominant elements of Byzantine civilization were Hellenistic and oriental. The tradition of classical Latin culture, the influence of which never died out in Western Europe, was but one of the intellectual factors to which Russia was not exposed until its contact with the West was intensified by Peter the Great at the beginning of the eighteenth century.

Another vital agent in Western civilization which never touched Russia directly was the complex of humanistic and renaissance ideals both in life and in literature. During the fourteenth century when the rising tide of humanism in Western Europe had revived the study of philosophy, politics, and science on the basis of classical sources, and when a fresh aesthetic pleasure was found not only in the imitation and the study of the ancients but also in the creation of new and popular forms in vernacular letters, Russia was just recovering from the economically destructive and intellectually paralyzing effects of the Tartar conquest which had weighed the nation down since 1240. Medieval Moscow had nothing of the thirst for knowledge and the ambition for culture that inspired the foundation of German universities during the last half of the fourteenth century. It lacked the close contacts with Italy of the sixteenth which meant for Western Europe the infusion of art into literature and bore fruit in France in the works of Ronsard and the Pléiade or in England in the brilliance of Spenser and Sidney. This heritage was transmitted to Russia only in the eighteenth century as an element in the literary models and traditions then taken over bodily from the West.

Apart from the classical tradition of the Middle Ages and the revival of intellectual and artistic creative fervor during the Renaissance, there was a third important element in Western culture to which Russia was not directly exposed: the spirit of the Protestant Reformation. Russia had received the Christian faith from Byzantium. But the Eastern Orthodox and the Western Roman Catholic Churches were split by the schism of 1054, sixty-five years after the conversion of Kiev. The Eastern Church intensified its emphasis on mysticism and asceticism without the balance of social and cultural interests which fertilized the labors of the Roman Church in Western Europe. Then, after the contacts between the Russian Church and Constantinople became difficult because of precarious communication, and still more after the fall of the Byzantine Empire fifty years before Columbus discovered America, the church in Russia became petrified in dogma and sunk in debased formalism. It maintained no such tradition of learning, no such cult of scholastic philosophy as made the Roman Church a nucleus of productive thought even in those periods of European political history in which popular culture was at its lowest ebb. It was incapable of producing such bold and independent thinkers as a Wyclif, a Hus, a Luther, or a Calvin. Indeed, had such thinkers arisen, it is doubtful whether, even in the church or among the limited section of the upper class which was literate, there could have been found a receptive public in whom their ideas could have taken root.

Thus, when the Byzantine intellectual influence (such as it was) died away, the Russian Church lost its function as a repository of culture, and never regained it before it was reduced to social impotence in our own day by revolutionaries angered at its pernicious coöperation with the autocracy. Nor had there ever arisen in Russia any fruitful movement of inspired protest on theological grounds which opposed the spirit of individual critical intelligence to the inertia of a dogma-ridden hierachy. All three of these crucial factors in the formation of the Western European outlook (the perpetuation of classical culture in the Middle Ages; humanism and the Renaissance; the Protestant Reformation) fall quite outside the purview of Russian intellectual life until introduced as contributing elements of the Western culture imposed upon Russia by Peter and his successors in the course of the eighteenth century.

When the Swedish warrior-merchants moved down the Russian watercourses, they established themselves as the economic and military ruling class in the small towns which the Eastern Slavs themselves had founded at strategic points for trade and defense. The impulse which first unified the Eastern Slavs into what eventually became the principality of Kiev resulted from the Varangian immigration, and though the immigrants were rapidly Russified by intermarriage with the native Slavs, the princes of Kiev still maintained intimate contact with Scandinavia. At the same time, their economic needs kept them in close relations with the Byzantine Empire for a century before the conversion of Kiev and for two centuries and a half thereafter.

Although Byzantine culture had its weaker aspects, we are too prone to underestimate its level and its service to the world, since nearly five centuries separate us from its collapse before the onslaught of the Turks. For while Western Europe was going through the painful process of civilizing the Germanic invaders as they fused with the native stocks, the Eastern Empire had grafted upon the legacy of Rome the picturesque and flamboyant features of oriental Christianity. Its autocratic sovereigns were the agents of God on earth under a system which combined in them the attributes of emperor and pope, and this factor ought especially to be borne in mind, because it not only explains the autocratic tradition later set up by the princes of Moscow but also lies at the root of the Russian tendency to attribute to all their rulers a sort of superhuman status. The superlative adulation showered on Joseph Stalin in our own day is in part a remote reflex of Byzantine influence. Then too, Constantinople before the arrival of the Crusaders was the greatest center of material civilization in the occidental world. Its buildings rivaled Rome in its prime. Its highly organized and stratified society, the splendor of its religious observances, its military prowess under the more gifted emperors, and its general atmosphere of wealth could not fail to create a lasting impression on visitors from less advanced regions.

But Byzantine civilization lacked the punch and the drive which characterized the best days of the Roman Empire or the realm of Charlemagne. In intellectual and literary matters the Eastern Empire was conservative. It studied the past without rivaling it with the products of contemporary creative imagination. It was compilatory rather than original. Byzantine scholars were the most learned men of their day, but their learning was accumulative, not productive. Byzantine historians composed voluminous chronicles without evolving a philosophy of history, while Byzantine theologians dissipated their energy on amenities of dogma argued with a bitterness which we should nowadays associate only with partisan politics. The Byzantine Church was more political than the Roman, more closely affiliated with the state, and hence less fundamentally spiritual in outlook. The literary tradition transmitted by the Byzantine Church was stiff and formalistic, and it was the misfortune of medieval Russia that the Byzantine influence was weakened by political events before it was absorbed by the younger state in a volume which might have served as a firm basis for the development of a characteristic native culture. The Russians before the Tartar invasion were always pupils; they originated very little that was independent of Byzantine models either in literature or in art.

In art, however, this imitation was productive and created an architectural and a decorative tradition which lasted down into modern times. By the date of Vladimir's conversion, the basilica as a type of church architecture in Byzantium had been largely replaced by the cruciform church with one or with five cupolas. This was the type transmitted to Russia and still worthily represented by the great medieval churches of Kiev, Novgorod, Vladimir and even Moscow, though in the metropolis the more exotic forms and the onion-shaped dome derived from wooden architecture prevail. The highly conventionalized art of the icon dominated Russian painting until Western influences began to seep in during the seventeenth century, but this tradition was still vital enough before the first World War to influence the art of nineteenth-century religious and historical painters. For where the Byzantine tradition had taken firm root, the aesthetic appeal was long-lived and enduring.

In literature, along with lapidary works of religious implication, the Russian national spirit began to manifest itself in historical compilations during the eleventh century, and literary reflexes of folk poetry had already appeared before the Tartar conquest. But a truly national literature stems from a long educative process, and this process was interrupted in medieval Russia both by domestic politics and by nomadic inroads.

Where domestic disorders merely retarded the intellectual advance of medieval Russia, the Tartar incursion brought it to a full stop. It has already been noticed what material impoverishment it had caused. But the Tartar domination was a far more serious factor in the deterioration of cultural and spiritual values. The church, to be sure, was treated with tolerance by the Tartars because it preached submission to the established authorities, and the princes, as we have seen, became Tartar vassals. In earlier days Byzantium had been at least a model to be emulated in material culture, literary and artistice endeavor, asceticism, and piety. But now central Russia was totally cut off from all contact with the West, while the Mongols, a seminomadic race which won new conquests by the aid of Turkic soldiery, promoted a lower level of political morality and a hypocritical subservience to alien authority which left an indelible print on the Russian character. The princes of Vladimir had always tended to be more absolutist than their Kievan forebears. Now the Tartar example ingrained in the Russian ruling classes a notion of tyranny and autocracy which became basic in the Muscovite state that rose more or less on the ruins of the Tartar khanates. Once this autocratic practice was later hallowed by the prestige of the Byzantine legacy and the conception of the divine rights of the prince or of the tsar of Muscovy, it was inevitable that an untrammeled throne with religious support would long be able to resist any but the most cataclysmic efforts to overthrow it.

The gap between the cultural levels of the Tartars and the Russians was too great to allow the Tartar domination to penetrate deeply into Russian life or to shake its foundation. Yet even contemporary monastic commentators were less impressed by material destruction and losses than by the lowering of the spiritual standard. The Tartars were not like the Spanish Moors, who bequeathed to their Spanish Christian subjects the relics of a highly developed Arab civilization. They were Asiatic nomads who preserved their semibarbarous existence unmodified. And among the fruits of their influence in Muscovite times may be numbered cruel torture, the use of the knout (the very name for whip in Russian, *nagaika,* is of Tartar origin), the relegation of women to haremlike seclusion which prevailed till Peter I's day, and the inconsiderate attitude of superior toward inferior which is the essence of tyranny.

We have seen how much interest the early Christian Kievan princes took in education, and the chronicles frequently characterize them as well-read and good linguists for their day and time. But during the Tartar hegemony such items are totally lacking. Not only the princes but even the higher clergy were frequently illiterate. Dmitri Donskoi could hardly read, and Basil II, Ivan the Terrible's great-grandfather, could neither read nor write. At the Council of Florence in 1439, Pope Eugene IV was told that the contemporary Russian bishops had little learning, and a feeble light of culture was kept burning in the Russian Church of this period solely by the appointment of Greek metropolitan bishops in Moscow. Only at the end of the fifteenth century do we encounter new interest in the foundation of schools for training the clergy, and considerable pressure in this direction was exercised by the Greek and South Slavic scholars who emigrated to Russia to escape the yoke of the Turks.

The advancement of clerical scholarship during the reign of Ivan III (1462-1505) was accompanied by a characteristic effort to acquire foreign techniques. Here, of course, we have an early example of what was to repeat itself so often in later days whenever the advancement of Russia required new mechanical skills. Under Ivan III Italian specialists were particularly active. The Bolognese architect Rudolfo Fioravanti not only built the Cathedral of the Assumption in the Kremlin, but also cast cannon, while Alevisio Novi, of Milan, designed and built the adjacent Cathedral of Saint Michael, in which were buried all subsequent Muscovite tsars to the time of Peter the Great. Miners, silversmiths, masons, and even an organist were imported from Hungary. Ivan the Terrible settled on the outskirts of Moscow in the so-called German suburb all German metalworkers who had been captured in his Livonian wars, and in 1567 obtained from England a doctor, an apothecary, and various goldsmiths. The Tsar was interested not only in material progress but also in raising the intellectual level of priests and officials, for it had been noted in the Church Council of 1551 that the opportunities for education were as yet slight. Besides, as the principality of Moscow developed into a national state and a world power, the need for trained personnel in the government services and in commerce became evident if only for practical considerations. Ivan the Terrible himself was comparatively well-educated, while Boris Godunov, his progressive but ill-fated minister and eventual successor, was obliged by the innate conservatism of the clergy to abandon a promising project for the establishment at Moscow of an academy with learned foreigners as teachers.

For, despite isolated outbreaks of rationalism which manifested themselves in heretical movements, the intellectual horizon of the Russian clergy was discouragingly narrow. After the Council of Florence, they considered themselves the sole repository of Orthodox rectitude and resented even competent criticism. That learned scholar from Mount Athos, Maxim Grek, who had studied in Italy and heard Savonarola preach, was accused of heresy and imprisoned when he ventured to suggest textual corrections of the accepted liturgy, and though he lived on into the reign of Ivan the Terrible, he was always regarded with suspicion and never allowed to return to his native country until his death in 1556.

Whatever material progress was registered under the Muscovite princes, the introduction of new intellectual concepts encountered serious barriers. From a social standpoint also the Muscovite regime was responsible for the establishment of one institution which cast its dark shadow over Russia far down into the nineteenth century. Though slavery was not unknown, universal agrarian serfdom does not date from the origins of Russia. On the contrary, its evolution was gradual. In the early Muscovite period there were two classes of peasants: first, those who had lived for some time on state, church, or private land and payed various fixed duties on the parcels they occupied; second, the so-called movable peasants who rented parcels on term contracts. As the princes assigned estates to deserving officials who did not belong to the old landed aristocracy, some competition developed among proprietors for peasants to till their lands, with the result that by the middle of the sixteenth century any transfer of the so-called fixed, or black, peasants was forbidden. The movable peasants, on the other hand, enjoyed the customary privilege of changing landlords when they desired. Ivan III's legislation thus guaranteed them the right to shift within the weeks on either side of St. George's day, in the autumn of each year, though the tax they paid for the enjoyment of the privilege was relatively high.

On the other hand, the need for help was so acute that landlords might frequently pay this tax and whatever other debts a movable peasant owed in order to induce him to settle on their estates, but a peasant not thus aided could no longer move and, if the advances received from his landlord in cash or kind were considerable, he too became permanently attached to the soil unless another landlord bailed him out. With increasing frequency, since a shift of landlord was rapidly becoming impossible, the peasants bound themselves not to withdraw, but to remain in permanent service under one master, under penalty of being returned by force in case they ever broke this contract. Apart from these developments, the fact that the majority of peasants had no capital whatever also tended to reduce to effective servitude such peasants as borrowed from landlords and bound themselves to serve the lender on his estate until the loan was liquidated. In principle such a borrower could free himself by paying the debt. In practice, however, all his labor was devoted to paying the interest rather than wiping out the capital, so that he never succeeded in liberating himself. The operation of this system was legally restricted during the sixteenth century, but it was at one with the other tendencies which contributed to immobilizing and enslaving a rural population which at its origins had been unattached and free. In the sixteenth century it was still free in theory, but in the seventeenth even this theoretical freedom vanished when the master wanted the peasant's labor and the government his taxes. To indemnify the landlord for his collective responsibility for the tax payments of the peasants on his estates, the latter were literally turned into the chattels of the landlord. In this way, under the early Romanovs, between 1630 and 1650, freedom of agricultural labor was abolished in Russia, and this situation prevailed until 1861.

The Muscovite system suffered a severe blow in 1598 when Theodore, Ivan the Terrible's son, died intestate and the old dynasty tracing its descent from Rurik became extinct. Since the realm and its inhabitants were regarded as the absolute property of the sovereign, the disappearance of the ruling family was a major catastrophe. Any tsar, however legitimately elected by the general assembly convoked by the patriarch of Moscow, was bound to be weakened by his dynastic illegitimacy. Hence with the reign of Boris Godunov began a period of violent revolution which lasted until 1613, largely motivated by the effort of the nobles to free themselves from exactions and restrictions which tradition forced them to endure from a scion of the old line, but which they would not suffer from anyone else.

When Michael, the first of the Romanovs, was finally elected to the throne in 1613, political self-consciousness had developed to the point where there was some realization that the sovereign actually depended on the people and not the reverse. On the other hand, this realization was strongest among the great nobles, the landowners, and the high officials, and they set up the new dynasty at the price of privileges not otherwise obtainable. It is also notable that the rudiments of parliamentary government, typified by a popular assembly, likewise existed in the early years of Michael's reign, but failed to mature because the level of popular political intelligence was not high enough to appreciate that elective representatives of the people had a real weapon in their potential control of finances. Hence there was no protest when the governing class allowed it to lapse. The government became intensely centralized, and with the establishment of serfdom the nobility and the gentry inevitably became a permanent ruling class upon which the crown was dependent. Since townsmen were forbidden to move into the country, and peasants could no longer establish themselves in the cities, there was as yet no prospect for the formation of a growing and self-conscious middle class whose aspirations might have sown the seeds of progress. As a result, during the seventeenth and eighteenth centuries all intellectual advance was confined to the aristocratic and ruling minority.

In the seventeenth century, however, the door was again opened to Western influence by the need for self-defense. Foreign mercenaries entered the Russian army, which now became a professional force. New mines and arsenals were opened. The foreign colony founded at Moscow by Ivan the Terrible (the German suburb), though scattered during the upheaval of 1598-1612, was soon repopulated with merchants, technicians, and artisans, and their advanced notions of material comfort influenced those Russians who came into contact with them. Artamon Matveycv, the able foreign minister of Michael's son, the Tsar Alexis (in turn Peter the Great's father), married a Scotch lady, and was one of the first Russian nobles to set up his household on a Western scale. Through him notions of contemporary culture penetrated even to the court. Natalia Narishkina, Peter the Great's mother, was Matveyev's ward, and though Scotch on her mother's side, was probably the first Muscovite lady of her day to receive even a moderate education and to emancipate herself from the seclusion in which noblewomen had vegetated since the Tartar conquest.

While material progress was largely implemented by the German technicians resident in Moscow, new theological and literary ideas penetrated the empire by another route. It may be recalled that Kiev and the Dnieper valley were conquered by the Lithuanians in 1363. Then by the fusion of Poland and Lithuania at the end of the fourteenth century, the whole Ukraine became exposed to Polish colonization and cultural influence. By the sixteenth century, Polish intellectual life was entirely under the control of the Jesuits, who developed an intense but largely unsuccessful proselytizing activity among the Orthodox Ukrainians. As a counterpoise against Jesuit influence, the Orthodox clergy of the Kiev area opened schools which taught the late renaissance disciplines on which the Poles themselves were fed. This process culminated in the establishment of a college at Kiev which was founded in 1622 by Peter Mogila, the great Orthodox Bishop of Kiev. An alumnus of this school, Simeon Polotski, who was already known to Tsar Alexis as a scholar and poet, migrated to Moscow in 1663, where he founded a small monastery school, and in 1667 became tutor to the Tsar's eldest son. Simeon was the first influential exponent at Moscow of renaissance scholarship on a Latin basis, and from 1667, when the Ukraine was ceded by Poland to Moscow, the impact of Western influences through Kievan channels was immediately intensified. That this infusion of a new spirit did not take place without violent opposition goes without saying, but destiny was on the side of the progressives, even though progress was appallingly slow.

It is apparent, however, that increasingly broader breaches had been splitting the Chinese Wall of Muscovite self-sufficiency ever since the time of Ivan III. But Peter the Great set out to demolish it with one charge. For a prince of Moscow, his upbringing was exceptional. His education had been fragmentary, but his free contacts with foreign technicians while he lived in the country near Moscow during the regency of his sister Sophia embued him with a profound taste for military and naval science and mechanics. Essentially practical and rationalistic, he departed from Muscovite tradition in caring nothing for the church as a vessel of dogma and used it only insofar as it was adaptable to his purposes. His boundless energy strained toward goals far beyond the comprehension of any but an infinitesimal minority of his subjects, the rest of whom he undertook to reform and modernize by brute force. But he knew Russia could not become a major European power without the knowledge by which to use the fruits of modern technique. This knowledge he literally drove into the Russians at the point of the bayonet. Since his eye was permanently fixed on material progress, he cared little for abstract learning. His idea of literature was propaganda, and the foreign works translated in his reign were mostly technical handbooks. He insisted on Western European costume, not from any aesthetic consideration, but because it was more practical and more comfortable to work in than the old Muscovite kaftan with its long sleeves. To prosecute his ends, he was obliged to create a bureaucracy whom he recruited from all strata of society, having little regard for origins if they were intelligent and efficient. Russian culture in Peter's day consisted of the tsar and his pathetically small group of specialists working at killing speed and pressure to overcome the national inertia.

But Peter abolished previous restrictions on foreign travel, and young aristocrats were sent abroad to study and to learn how the Europeans actually lived. The tsar traveled in foreign countries himself. Foreign specialists entered the Russian service in unparalleled numbers. His reign brought to light no liberal tendencies, however, since the nobility absorbed the new bureaucracy and strengthened its hold on the national substance. Yet the channel was opened for a new complex of ideas. Peter forced his subjects to go abroad to study engineering and anatomy, and they observed humanity and the mechanism of states. Unsuccessful attempts to limit the absolute power of the throne were made immediately after Peter's death in 1725.

New notions of the amenities of social intercourse and of the pleasures offered by arts, music, the dance, and literature were added to Peter's more materialistic innovations when his daughter Elizabeth came to the throne in 1741, with the result that French civilization acquired a dominance in Russian intellectual life which it began to lose only at the beginning of the nineteenth century. The origins of the Russian ballet go back to 1735, in the reign of Elizabeth's cousin Anna, who also introduced Italian opera, but the French theater reached St. Petersburg in Elizabeth's reign, which also witnessed the beginnings of the native Russian drama composed in the French pseudoclassic vein of Corneille, Racine, and Molière.

Russian poets with more form than talent now began to celebrate official occasions and generous donors with ponderous odes. Handbooks of French pseudoclassic literary theory, like Boileau's *Art Poétique,* were translated and annotated. The Academy of Sciences, founded by Peter's widow in 1725, included not only imported German luminaries, but the first Russian natural scientist Michael Lomonosov, sometimes characterized as the Russian Franklin, but whom, on account of the universality of his talent, Pushkin, greatest of Russian poets, called "Russia's first university." He is also notable as the first proletarian in secular Russian letters, for he started his career as a poor fisherman's son far north on the White Sea. The first modern Russian history was composed during the reigns of Anna and Elizabeth by Basil Tatishchev, a former collaborator of Peter the Great. The purely intellectual progress in the thirty years after Peter's death was thus considerable, even though (with rare exceptions) it was confined to the aristocracy.

It is a matter of record that when Catherine II came to the throne in 1762 she was already familiar with the theories of the eighteenth-century French political philosophers and would have welcomed an opportunity to apply them. But her position had been won wholly by the aid of the landed gentry and the aristocratic guard regiments, who were unlikely to surrender any of their prerogatives or to consent to any mitigation of the institution of serfdom on which their economic existence was based. The great empress thus contributed little to social progress, and her educational innovations remained for the most part on paper. Yet through her interest in the satirical journal and in the drama, she stimulated the progress of Russian letters even if her social initiatives were weak. In that field others carried the torch. A Russian customs official, Alexander Radishchev, who had studied at Leipzig and digested the liberal philosophy of the day, in 1780 fired the opening gun against serfdom, and though the exploit sent him to Siberia, its echoes did not die away until the institution was abolished. At the same time, the spirit of social service inspired the idealistic Freemasons, whose leader, Nicholas Novikov, as a humanitarian publicist, founded lending libraries and endowed with textbooks the rudimentary schools of the day, even though he too paid for this initiative by long imprisonment after the French Revolution closed Catherine's mind to liberal ideas. The spirit of satire also awoke, and inspired Denis Fonvisin's two masterly comedies in which the brutality and backwardness of the lower nobility and the venality of the state administration were bitterly attacked. These men foreshadow the role of nineteenth-century Russian literature as an organ of protest and an instrument of reform.

By the end of the eighteenth century, the stiffness of the French pseudoclassic influence began to retreat before new currents deriving from German and English literature, which give more play to individual self-expression and concerned themselves not so much with any aristocratic ideal as with the fortunes and the betterment of the common man. Through sentimentalism Russian authors graduated from the mere imitation of form to the expression of a new national spirit. Under the influence of French prose style, the literary language now attained a flexibility and a force fully comparable to that of other vernaculars, and within a decade or more after 1800 a few talented poets had adapted to Russian every verse form practiced by the German poets of the *Sturm und Drang* period and of the various romantic schools.

The tempo of Russian social thought and literary expression from this point forward keeps pace with the rapid evolution of European history. In Peter the Great's day and during the first half of Catherine II's reign, the throne had stood in the vanguard of progress. But vested interests rarely move as fast as the most gifted and public-spirited thinkers. When Catherine died in 1796, even her own Russian world had passed her by, and during the entire nineteenth century until 1917 the autocracy continued futile efforts to delay a process which no official hand could stay. In the course of the Napoleonic wars, the young Russian officers who participated in Western European campaigns were inoculated with the republican ideas disseminated by the French revolution. Essentially patriotic, they were eager to apply these ideals to their own country, to abolish the autocracy, promote republican government, raise the standard of education, and do away with the abuses of serfdom. They continued with greater energy, though often with little judgment, the task begun by Radishchev.

Here the Russian revolutionary movement begins among an enlightened fraction of the ruling class. Great writers like Pushkin and Lermontov, each after brief romantic digressions, grew up to treat the seamy side of reality, both in the tragedy of the humble who are scarcely considered human by those they serve, or the misfortune of the gifted individual denied a chance at productive activity by the contemporary organization of society. Both these talents were suspected and harassed by the autocracy, and though each met his death in a duel, they were as truly victims of official conservatism as those young enthusiasts who had participated in the Decembrist conspiracy in 1825 after the death of Alexander I, and paid for it on the scaffold or amid the snows of Siberia. But from 1825 the cleavage between the government and the thoughtful section of society, once opened, was never bridged again.

This mutual hostility first became acute during the reign of Nicholas I from 1825 to the Crimean War. The Decembrist conspiracy had revealed that the turn to the right by Alexander I after 1815 had created great bitterness. The same judicial and administrative abuses that marred Catherine's reign were still rampant, state finances were disordered, and the peasants were rudely exploited. Nicholas at first had some notion of reform, but his suspicion of extragovernmental initiative was such that he hesitated to take any concrete step. The most pressing problem was serfdom: the landlords were heavily in debt and short of capital to provide employment for a rapidly increasing peasant population. Peasant disorders were menacingly frequent, but only in the western Ukraine and in Poland were reforms introduced. Educational institutions were fettered and muzzled lest they should become centers of liberal thought, but in spite of galling restrictions they performed precisely this function.

In the presence of such challenging problems, sociological reflection was inevitable. At the University of Moscow, a brilliant group of young students absorbed the philosophy of Hegel and were attracted by the utopian socialism of Saint-Simon. From 1840-1880 Russian authors were rare who had not been touched by the socialist idea. Of the younger generation, Belinski, the father of systematic Russian literary criticism, Bakunin, once a friend of Karl Marx and later an active anarchist, and Herzen, the father of Russian revolutionary journalism, all passed through this school. The place of Russia in European civilization was actively debated. The so-called "Westerners," hateful of the autocracy under which they lived, demanded that Russia should complete the common course of European political and social evolution, but at an accelerated speed. The socialists thus hoped that Russia might skip entirely or escape in large degree the injustices and errors of the bourgeois system. The Slavophiles, with more romantic loyalty, believed that Russia should follow a special path which they deduced from a mistaken interpretation of medieval Russian social conditions. Turgenev, the great novelist, dedicated his youthful career to the destruction of serfdom. These liberal aspirations were rudely interrupted by a stiffening of government resistance after the revolutionary events of 1848, but were merely driven to cover. The Crimean War revealed all the weaknesses of the autocracy, and the reign of Alexander II after 1855 saw not only the emancipation of the peasants but a large and promising body of administrative reforms.

The greatest age of Russian letters extends from 1855 to the death of Dostoevski in 1881. Sociological criticism inspired by socialist ideals defined the role of literature. The spirit of realism, established by Gogol in the forties was perpetuated by Turgenev in his portrayals and criticisms of the rising nihilistic generation, suspicious of all beliefs of their fathers, and in his pictures of the decaying landed gentry. Goncharov composed the classic of Russian imagination paralyzed by inertia. Tolstoi studied the peasant problem, painted the first twenty years of the century on the magnificent canvas of his *War and Peace,* and returned to contemporary agrarian and urban problems with *Anna Karenina.* Dostoevski, after poignantly describing the bitter life of the humble in *Poor People,* acquired still deeper sympathy in his exile, and having expounded his doctrine of atonement through suffering in *Crime and Punishment,* attacked the radicals in *The Possessed,* and revealed the whole scope of his psychological penetration and the breadth of his religious philosophy in *The Brothers Karamazov.* With other authors of scarcely less merit describing contemporary life, these three decades constitute an outburst of brilliance unequaled in any world literature. Russian verse of the period was no less meritorious, and even Russian painters chose subjects which reflected the contemporary state of mind.

While the aims of political and social thinkers expanded, the tempo of the reforms gradually slowed down with dangerous results. Active revolutionary groups had begun to take shape even in the heyday of reform, and strove for rapid democratization in the public interest. Even in the fifties, literature had ceased to be an exclusive perquisite of the aristocracy and was professionally practiced by many young men from the new middle class who were impatient at the slowness of change. Some of the young radicals made unfruitful efforts to form a community of interest with the peasantry. Others attempted to force the hand of the government by acts of violence. Marxist socialism became known in Russia during the seventies and, while it supplied the young radicals with a more aggressive program, it suggested a transfer of their missionary efforts from the peasants to the urban industrial workers who were expanding in numbers with the progressive industrialization of the country.

The rising tide of radicalism stimulated repressive measures by the government, which gradually lost much of the sympathy which it had previously enjoyed in more moderate spheres, and even rejected loyal proposals for conservative reforms advanced in order to discourage the repeated outrages of the terrorists. In 1880 the situation came to a head with an explosion in the Winter Palace itself at St. Petersburg in which the whole imperial family narrowly escaped a violent death. Alexander II then called liberal statesmen who enjoyed the public confidence to work out a series of innovations which, though not aiming at a constitution, were at least conciliatory and progressive. These reforms were viewed with apprehension by the radicals, who not only feared to lose their public but also believed (mistakenly, as it proved) that the elimination of the tsar would be the prelude to a great popular uprising. They thus assassinated Alexander II on March 13, 1881.

The results were devastating. Moderate opinion was profoundly shocked, the government relapsed into a reactionary policy which endured until 1917, only briefly interrupted by the revolution of 1905. Political freedom and even political thought were discouraged, and many conscientious liberals were reduced to disillusion and despair by the bitter conviction that progress was impossible. The situation was not helped by the economic crisis of the eighties which followed an inflationary period of hasty industrial overexpansion.

This disillusion is most clearly reflected in the dramas of Chekhov, those twilight pictures of a class which vegetates without hope of change, without faith in its capacity to influence events. To this situation the accession of Nicholas II in 1894 brought no cure; since he was largely surrounded by ministers who deprecated even local self-government as only a step toward constitutionalism. But beneath the surface a new spirit was about to break ground. Some of the younger generation could no longer accept the resignation which Chekhov's characters practiced. For them, failure, however tragic, was not an everlasting stop-signal. Marxism gave them a program and a method. It warned them not to expect salvation from the middle class, and preached the virtues and strength of the so

Foundations of Russian Culture

far silent but ambitious proletariat. The lower strata of society were no longer looking for sympathy. They wanted power, and if properly led would break down all barriers to its attainment. The voice of the grumbling dispossessed first sounded clearly in Russian literature through Maxim Gorki's early stories, which began to appear in 1892. The best example of the young intellectual who discovered saving graces in Marxism was Lenin. He began to study Marx's *Capital* in 1888, organized a group of Marxists at Kuibyshev (Samara) in 1893, and was a social-democratic propagandist in St. Petersburg the next year. The emergence of Marxism as an active political and economic system in Russia dates from this period.

The rise of the Social Democratic party and the foundation of the more activist section known as the Bolsheviki (the maximalists) headed by Lenin himself preceded the outbreak of the Russo-Japanese war by barely one year. At the same time, another radical party, the Social Revolutionaries, revived the tradition of terrorism as practiced before the assassination of Alexander II in 1881. The government pursued a policy of repression even when the necessity of prosecuting a war for which the nation was totally unprepared might well have dictated a more conciliatory attitude. Profound resentment now mastered not only the middle class but the urban proletariat, and though the police resorted to desperate provocatory acts in order to discredit the agitators, a united front against the government was rapidly forming. When open revolution broke out early in 1905, neither the middle-class liberals nor the radical Marxist groups possessed an organization equal to organizing and directing a mass movement. As a result, after the government made various constitutional concessions and the extremists showed every sign of fighting to a finish, the moderate groups gravitated away from the revolutionary idea, leaving the Marxist leaders and the workers isolated. With the urban middle class again passive, the government speedily recovered its sangfroid and applied repressive measures of forbidding severity which were far from supplying any basis for reconciliation with society. The new parliament was never allowed to function efficiently, and excessive parcellation of parties within it also prevented the formation of a workable united front against the government, though the fundamental tone was one of hostility.

The first World War began in this atmosphere of mutual distrust between government and society, and only a brief interval of patriotic *entente cordiale* intervened before official incompetence as revealed by repeated military defeats once more opened the breach, which was further widened by a complete collapse of transportation and economic life. General resentment was intensified by evidence of a total lack of comprehension of the situation by the tsar and his advisers, and culminated in the events of March, 1917, by which the tsar was forced to abdicate and a democratic regime was set up. The vacillations of successive moderate provisional governments played into the hands of the Bolshevik leaders, who could always bank on the support of the urban factory workers and certain sections of the army, and on November 7 they were masters of Petrograd. The subsequent fortunes of the Soviets are so close to our own times as to be matters of common knowledge.

The chasm which existed between government and society between 1894 and the first World War did not prevent simultaneous developments in Russian intellectual life. In spite of government surveillance and occasional restriction of educational facilities, a highly educated and talented middle class had evolved in Russia during the last quarter of the nineteenth century. Though literature declined in some degree after the death of Dostoevski, Tolstoi lived on to combine moral philosophy and creative letters until 1910. Chekhov's later plays expressed his own prevision that an epoch was about to end. A younger generation of prose writers revived traditional Russian realism in a more individualistic spirit without regard to the political and social aims that had inspired their predecessors. In poetry, symbolism sought to penetrate and express deeper

Foundations of Russian Culture

elements of truth which lay behind the veil of everyday reality as presented to the senses. In painting, the social angle and exclusively realistic technique were abandoned for impressionism and the development of stage decoration. The romantic ballet which had dominated the theater for half a century was replaced by the more plastic creations of Diagilev and his group. In almost every phase of intellectual life Russia had now joined Europe and in music and the arts of the theater was rapidly assuming a position of leadership, while Russian scientists, though usually trained in French or German schools, originated theories and techniques which still influence modern scientific practices and conceptions. The Russian schools of historians and philologists were on a par with those of countries whose culture was the result of much longer growth to the point where several of us at Harvard are proud to acknowledge our debt to these masters. Whatever the backwardness of the Russian political system, the old empire at last came to possess an intellectual minority which in gifts and productivity was without superior in the history of modern civilization.

Yet at best it was a minority, and the mass of the population, especially in the rural districts and among the numerous non-Slavic elements, participated but remotely in its eminence. The task of spreading European culture to the masses thus devolved upon the Soviet government as soon as it had consolidated its position and reëstablished some semblance of ordered political and economic life. Even if we admit that the rise of Soviet culture is hampered by communist ideology, especially in the social sciences, the fact remains that the progress of popular education under Soviet auspices deserves the respect and gratitude of the world at large. Illiteracy, once a curse, has been stamped out in the cities and greatly reduced in the countryside. Though the caliber of the teaching staff in higher institutions of learning has obviously been reduced by political factors, access to technical schools and universities is now open to a class whose representatives could barely walk past their entrances in the old imperial days. Linguistic minorities which never even had alphabets, let alone schools, now have both. Their cultural representatives are hailed as contributors to the intellectual life of the nation, which has a chance of not remaining purely Slavic or European, but may instead draw new life and inspiration from the resident Asiatic and other alien stocks. The intermediate and elementary school system has been extended into the most remote districts, and in non-Slavic areas the native tongue has an equal chance with the official Russian.

The pressure of doctrine which long lay heavy on literature and art, however, has been intensified in recent years. The trend of the times is naturally in favor of a somewhat romantic and dogmatic picture of reality, since it would not be in the interest of the prevailing system to admit that its present imperfections are permanent departures from the ideal which has been set up. Present-day Soviet culture is intensely patriotic, not to say nationalistic. But of the great legacy of the nineteenth century surprisingly little has been lost. The classics are the models for present-day writers. But upon the accomplishment of the past have been grafted the materialistic aims of a new society which aims at a degree of organization and technical achievement which even the great progressives of the sixties would not have deemed possible. For though the autocracy of the Soviet State echoes more than once the spirit of the Muscovite Middle Ages and sometimes applies the methods of the Tartars for its self-preservation, the fact still remains that this autocracy is inwardly devoted to a program of national service, the execution of which we may only hope will not be too seriously hampered or interrupted by international factors and power politics which divert national energy and resources from domestic growth and construction to baser military ends.

VI

German and Slav

While speaking of the process by which the Western and some of the Southern Slavs were converted to Christianity, it has been mentioned that German missionary efforts were accompanied by widespread colonization not only along the Danube but likewise in Central Germany itself. It may be recalled also that, after the Germanic migrations, the Slavs by the sixth century had expanded from their former boundary at the Vistula westward to the Elbe and simultaneously occupied the Baltic coast from the peninsula of Jutland eastward to the former Polish corridor. While they were in Bohemia and Moravia, as well as in the Vistula basin, they set up large and comparatively strong Slavic social and political organizations which, despite many handicaps, have maintained themselves down into modern history. But the Slavs who occupied the course of the Elbe and the Baltic seaboard formed nothing more than weak tribal federations which not only possessed little internal cohesion but also collapsed easily at any external shock. At the same time the Slavs south of the Danube, and especially the Slovenes, were unable to form lasting ties with any more powerful Slavic group which would guarantee them against German pressure and infiltration; consequently they were gradually forced to contract into their present restricted frontiers.

Along the Danube the banner of German expansion was carried by the Bavarians. They were the descendants of the powerful tribe of the Marcomanni, whose prowess taxed the arms of Marcus Aurelius in the second century. The earliest known German habitat of the Bavarians was between the Saale river and the Bohemian border, from which they spread southward to the Danube and then followed its course eastward into upper Austria, the Salzburg area, and the Tyrol. Their nominal submission to the Franks in the sixth century was inspired by the same Avar menace which in turn dictated the surrender of the Slovenes in Carinthia to the Bavarians a hundred years later. The Bavarians themselves were Christianized only in the seventh century. Salzburg, their first bishopric, was founded in 696, but before the Bavarians were completely subjugated by Charlemagne in 788 their country was already swarming with Benedictine cloisters. German colonization of the middle Danube basin was thus primarily monastic and aristocratic. The Slovenian villages maintained but a precarious existence among the lands of newly established monasteries and of German settlers imported en masse from the valleys of the Rhine and the Moselle to clear and work the estates of immigrant proprietors.

After the Avars, the chief impediment to peaceful penetration along the Danube, had been defeated by Charlemagne in his campaigns of 791-796, he founded the Ostmark, which immediately became the goal of intensively organized colonization and eventually developed into the Duchy of Austria. Though the German advance had crossed the Danube into modern Hungary by the last decade of the ninth century, its progress was halted in 881 by the invasion of the Magyars, who defeated the Bavarians at Bratislava in 907, and for the next forty-five years repeatedly devastated the Ostmark until they were repulsed by Otto I on the Lechfeld, near Augsburg, in 955. From this moment, despite occasional Magyar raids, colonization was resumed along the right bank of the Danube between

Passau and Vienna, and the area devastated by the Magyars was largely reoccupied by the year 1000.

At this period, German missionary work in the Slavic districts south of the Danube proceeded not from Regensburg or Passau, which were mainly occupied with the German settlements along the Danube, but from Bamberg. Missionaries from this diocese lived among the Slavs of Carinthia which was rapidly settled by colonists from Franconia and the middle Rhineland, as opposed to the predominantly Bavarian origin of the German settlers in Austria itself. While Bamberg was thus active in Carinthia (roughly the valley of the Drave east and west of Villach), Bavarian missionaries from Freising in Bavaria occupied themselves with Carniola (Krain), the region of the Save valley somewhat further southwest (the hinterland of Trieste), and here the colonists were again Bavarian. The Slovene population found by these German newcomers in Carinthia, Carniola, and Styria (originally a portion of Carinthia), was less driven out or exterminated than it was repressed. Documentary evidence reveals German and Slavic personal and place names side by side. The politically and socially dominant class was everywhere German. In Austria along the Danube, from which the Slavic population had been driven by the Avars before Carolingian times, the peasantry was almost exclusively Bavarian. But in Carinthia and Carniola, German peasants lived in close proximity to the native Slovenian peasantry which remained most numerous southwest of the Mur river in the valleys of the Drave and Save. Peculiar conditions on the right bank of the Danube thus explain the southward contraction of the Slovenes away from this river and their constant subservience in later days to Austrian political influence.

German influences in Moravia and their unfortunate consequences for the mission of Constantine and Methodius have already been mentioned. Even while the brothers were still active, the struggle for Frankish supremacy was going on and by 874 the vassalage of Moravia was definitely established. After the epoch of Constantine and Methodius, all prospect of Moravian independence was destroyed by the Magyar invasion of the year 900, and for a century this region remained under Hungarian control until it was acquired by Bohemia in 1003. The decline of Moravia was paralleled by the rise of Bohemia. Early in the ninth century Charlemagne had invaded Bohemia, and in 849 the Bavarian Nordgau was founded as a barrier against the Czechs. This same epoch witnessed a gradual consolidation of the Czech cantons into a single state, as well as the baptism of numerous Czech notables at Regensburg. By the close of the ninth century, Bohemia became a vassal state of Germany and a part of the Regensburg diocese. German colonization into the district of Eger, only recently a bone of contention between the Czechs and Germans, began early in the tenth century, and paralleled Bavarian aggression on the southwestern frontier. The first half of that century was signalized by repeated German invasions of Bohemia from the north, and the situation was not stabilized until 971 when, under Otto I, the first Bohemian bishopric was established at Prague and subordinated to the Archbishop of Mainz. Soon thereafter Benedictine monasteries were founded, and aristocratic Czech circles were rapidly imbued with German culture.

Contacts between Czechs and Germans were intensified all during the eleventh century. German colonists (traders, farmers, technicians) arrived in large numbers. The annual fair at Prague came to be dominated by resident German merchants who occupied a position of virtual extraterritoriality, having their own magistrates and living under German law. Benedictine foundations were supplemented by Premonstratensian and Cistercian religious houses, who competed with their predecessors for privileges and donations. The mountainous parts of Bohemia were not opened to German colonization until nearly 1200 when numerous German settlers moved in through the Eger valley, and during the next century the Germans settled the southern, western, and eastern frontiers of

Bohemia. Sometimes a Bohemian village received so many German colonists that it was practically changed into a German settlement. Czech towns frequently were obliged to alter their traditional character and adopt German usages. The nobles began to resurvey and repartition the lands attached to these villages, forcing the Czech peasants to pay rent and to assume all obligations applied to the newer settlers. The Czechs were obliged to accept these innovations for fear of being dispossessed in favor of the German newcomers, and this process continued until the early fifteenth century and the period of the Hussite Wars.

The Germanization of Bohemia progressed most rapidly after the year 1200. King Václav (Wenceslas) I was a great friend of the German colonists, even to the point of driving the Czech peasants out of his native town and settling it with Germans, and his example was eagerly followed by the Bohemian nobility. It even became the custom to rechristen local castles with German names and to give new ones such names to start with, till the country bristled with Löwenbergs, Steinbergs, Rosenbergs, and Rosenthals. New monasteries were headed by German abbots who systematically forgot the Old Slavonic liturgy and the great tradition of Methodius, though he was buried at Velehrad, from 1201 the site of a Cistercian house. Among the German militant orders, the Knights of St. John were permitted to settle German colonists anywhere upon their lands. These settlers were exempt from local laws and freed from local duties and obligations. Both Templars and Hospitallers had established churches at Prague before 1255. About the same period, Dominicans and Franciscans also founded their first Bohemian houses, including both German and Italian friars. The German colony at Prague was the oldest and richest foreign group within the country, since all other German settlements were either in rural districts or in the mountainous mining regions.

The favors extended to the Germans at Prague were not dictated by sentiment but by practical interests, since they insured the commercial and economic prosperity of the country. The section of Prague now known as the Old Town was by the year 1200 almost wholly occupied by Germans, and was fortified by its own wall and moat. German law, craftsmanship, and commercial ability were particularly fruitful in the development of provincial civic centers during the twelfth century, and in the next hundred years they attained a high level of prosperity with flourishing handicrafts and agriculture. Their trade relations extended to Venice, Rome, Hamburg, Brandenburg, and Flanders; the primary article of Bohemian export was textiles. German colonization not only founded towns but also increased the number of free farmers. These German rural colonists were most interested in the settlement of the less fruitful districts, especially in the forests of the western and northern borders of Bohemia. Since the development of this land required much hard work, the native Czech peasantry had never been intensely concerned with it, and it therefore yielded no profit to the landlords until the Germans began to exploit it. Hence the colonists received attractive terms in the guise of local self-government and tax exemptions in order to induce them to take it up. These circumstances thus favored extensive German settlement in the border districts simultaneously with the evolution of a prosperous and wealthy German middle class in the growing Bohemian cities.

It is important to dwell on these conspicuous factors in the early development of Bohemia in order to show that the German penetration into this basically Slavic area occurred far back in the Middle Ages and is by no means a situation of recent growth. Since German settlements in the frontier districts actually took up land which the Czechs themselves had never occupied, any attempt to establish the frontiers of Czechoslovakia only on strategic considerations without regard to the conditions under which the country developed simply did violence to history and was inevitably destined to provoke discord. Whatever one may think of Nazi policy toward Czechoslovakia, the fact remains that the Germans had contributed just as much to the building up of Bohemia as did the Czechs. Apart from the early conflicts by which Bohemia became a German vassal, the colonists were brought into the country voluntarily by Bohemian princes and barons, and they could therefore hardly be regarded in our own time as an inferior element with restricted rights in an area to whose economic and cultural development they had been generously contributing for seven hundred years.

It is fair to observe, however, that internal conflict between Czech and German broke out at the time of the Hussite Wars of the fifteenth century. The radical Hussites bitterly attacked the German population, which was in the main composed of faithful Catholics, and even wiped out the entire German citizenry of numerous cities and towns, while such German residents who compounded with the Hussite extremists were subjected to a violent campaign of Czechization. The results of this epoch of conflict were catastrophic. Most of what the German element jointly with the Bohemian had built up in three centuries of faithful effort was destroyed in less than half a century during which the Czechs split with the Germans on account of their loyal Catholicism. The weakness of the Hussite movement was that, while doubtless promoting a healthy national spirit, it broke down the traditional contacts which in previous centuries had contributed appreciably to the advance of culture and to the international prestige of the nation. The succession to the Bohemian crown first passed to the house of Austria in 1437, and Bohemia subsequently remained under the sovereignty of the Hapsburgs uninterruptedly from 1526 to 1918. During this period of nearly three hundred years there was obviously little doubt of the dominance of German influence.

Before turning to early German relations with the rising Polish state, let us follow the fortunes of the Slavs who emigrated westward to the basin of the Elbe. While the burden of German colonization on the Danube front was carried by the Bavarians with some aid from the Franconians, the same function was performed in north central Germany by the Saxons. The first thrust of Slavic westward pressure had been felt in the fifth century by the Thuringians, whom the Slavs drove westward into the Thuringian forest and the Harz Mountains. As soon as the Thuringians were subjected by the Franks, the age of Slavo-German conflict set in, and hostilities were intermittent in eastern Franconia during the seventh century. Then, in the eighth century, the establishment of numerous monastery-fortresses on the frontier between the Danube and the Weser heralded an aggressive German offensive which developed as soon as the Franks in 804 had conquered the great tribal duchy of Saxony in lower Germany between the Elbe and the Rhine. The German *Drang nach Osten* which resulted in the dispossession and practical extermination of the Slavs on north-German soil thus began in Charlemagne's day, and continued for nearly four hundred years. Charlemagne opened the contest in 789 by attacking the Wilzi, a federation of Slavic tribes residing east of the Elbe in the vicinity of modern Berlin, and their spirited resistance induced him to give his eastern frontier a solid military organization. New fortresses were built on the lower Elbe to protect Saxony from Slavic invasion. Under Louis the Pious, Hamburg and Würzburg became advance posts of German missionary activity, but the last half of the ninth century witnessed almost constant warfare along the Slavo-German frontier from Hamburg to Bohemia, and these border clashes were a fruitful source of slave labor for the vast properties of the new German monasteries of the eastern front.

In 919, with the election of Duke Henry of Saxony as King of the Germans and successor to Conrad I, the last of the Carolingians, the period of large-scale Saxon aggression against the north German Slavs began. The first Saxon conquest recovered the area between the Saale and the upper Elbe, roughly between modern Halle and Meissen. Then, in the winter of 928-929, Henry pushed across the Elbe and captured Branibor, the stronghold of the Slavs on the Havel west of

Berlin, transforming it into a fortress which is the ancestor of modern Brandenburg. A Slavic coalition inspired by this offensive was defeated in 929 near Wittenberg, and the Saxon sphere of influence was thus extended to the Oder river. While Henry I showed little interest in colonizing the area he had won, and was solely concerned with collecting tribute, a movement of colonization was first reflected by a large number of fortified German settlements established east of the lower Elbe under Henry's successor Otto I, and a similar practice prevailed further south in the reconquered territory between the Saale and the upper Elbe. The German treatment of their Slavic subjects was far from gentle: captives taken in war were ruthlessly butchered, and chieftains invited as guests were treacherously slain. As a result, a Slavic revolt of 983 threw the Saxons out of Brandenburg. For a hundred and fifty years the Slavic coastal area from Lübeck to the Oder was thus free of Saxon encroachment, and it was not until after 1125 that the linguistic frontier in this region advanced beyond where it had stood in Charlemagne's day.

With the election of Duke Lothar of Saxony as King of the Germans in 1125, the situation altered. Even before his accession to the throne, Lothar had been known to the Slavs as a dangerous adversary, and no such drastically anti-Slavic policy as his had been seen since Henry the Fowler two hundred years before. His collaboration with the Danes broke up the Slavic principalities on the Baltic shore east of Holstein, and after Lothar's death in 1137 the coastline between Kiel and Rostock was soon in German hands. Wholesale colonization by Westphalian and other Low-German settlers immediately ensued under reasonably peaceful conditions, which unfortunately were interrupted by a fanatical crusade against the Slavs in 1147, in the vicissitudes of which most of the newly won territory was cruelly devastated. The result was thirty years of conflict in which the last independent group of Baltic Slavs was obliterated. Meanwhile Brandenburg had come back under German control when its Slavic chief died intestate in 1150 and willed his holdings to the neighboring German margrave. German influence was thus restored in this area to the Oder frontier which it had temporarily reached two hundred years before.

Albert von Ballenstedt, called "the Bear," Margrave of the Nordmark, into whose hands Brandenburg fell by legacy, is the most sympathetic figure of the German colonization period. He refused to participate in the Wendish crusade of 1147, and thus won the confidence of his Slavic subjects. Brandenburg was free from the trivial and exasperating obligations that weighed upon the peasantry of the older settled regions. There were no traditional rights and no antiquated feudal interests, with the result that as population increased in the west, pioneer colonization toward the east was intensified. The analogy is frequently drawn between this medieval German colonization of the eastern marches and the American migration west of the Alleghenies at the beginning of the nineteenth century. As one French historian wrote in 1875, "the German emigrant in the Middle Ages went beyond the Elbe in order to find free land as today he is crossing the Atlantic." Albert himself died in 1170, but well into the thirteenth century, under his successors, this colonization moved on toward the Polish borderland, and Frankfurt on the Oder was founded in 1253.

As a matter of fact, German contacts with Poland date back to the latter part of the reign of Otto I, who occupied the German throne from 936 to 973. Under Otto I the German margrave subjugated the Slavs of Lusatia, and extended his sway into Lower Silesia as far as the Bober river, but when one of his successors somewhat later endeavored to extend German influence east of the Oder into Polish territory, he was thrown back in 979. As it was mentioned in dealing with the conversions of the various Slavic nations, Prince Mieszko I of Poland had abandoned paganism in 966 upon his marriage to Dubravka, sister of the Bohemian prince Boleslav I, and three years later founded the bishopric of Posen, which was dependent upon the archdiocese of Magdeburg. On Easter Day 973, Mieszko, together with his Czech brother-in-law, was present as a vassal at Otto I's court in Quedlinburg. In spite of varying fortunes, the Polish ruler subsequently remained a reasonably faithful feudatory of the Saxon emperors until his own death in the summer of 992.

His son Boleslav the Brave at first pursued the same policy, aiding Otto III against the rebellious Elbian Slavs in 994-995. But he subsequently rewarded himself for this aid by stretching his own territory westward to the Bober, and was on sufficiently good terms with Otto to receive his visit to Gnesen in the year 1000 and to see his capital raised to an archbishopric. Then, after Otto's death in 1002, while internal difficulties occupied his successor, Boleslav calmly appropriated the whole march of Meissen east of the Elbe and even subjugated Moravia. For the next decade all efforts to pry Boleslav loose from his gains proved unavailing, and it was only in 1013 that he made peace with Henry II because he had ambitious plans connected with the succession of Vladimir I of Kiev, whose son Boleslav's daughter had married. Later, by the Peace of Bautzen, concluded in 1018, Boleslav guaranteed himself the possession of Lusatia, thus biting still deeper into the march of Thuringia, and it was only in 1031 that Conrad II managed to drive the Poles out of it and to restore Poland to a state of vassalage.

The next two hundred years were marked by a serious decline in the energy and authority of the Polish state, caused by the weakness of its princes and the long struggle for domination between the throne on one hand and the magnates and the clergy on the other. It should be noted that the early clerics in Poland were mainly foreigners of either German or Bohemian birth. They held their charges directly from the king or prince and represented a stage in the administrative hierarchy, making the church an official institution. The clergy in general was supported by a tithe from villages and counties.

The monasteries were, on the whole, the only large private landowners, and supplied an example by their organization of large manors worked by half-free peasants.

With the throne weakened by the pretensions of the Polish nobility, an aggressive foreign policy was unthinkable. After Vladislav Hermann accepted the status of a German vassal in 1080, no Polish prince dared assume the title of king for two centuries. The Elbe valley and Silesia were definitely lost, together with the Pomeranian seaboard west of the Vistula. Then, early in the thirteenth century, when the still pagan Prussians menaced Duke Conrad of Mazovia (along the Vistula northwest of Warsaw) he turned for aid to the knights of the Teutonic Order, who entered Mazovia and occupied the districts ceded to them in 1229. They immediately founded strong points at Thorn, Kulm, Elbing and elsewhere, and by placing themselves under papal protection obviated any chance of Polish sovereignty. The next fifty years were occupied by the struggle of the Teutonic Order, supported by the margraves of Brandenburg and Meissen, against the Prussians. Königsberg was founded in 1255, when the Slavic Duke of Pomerelia, on the lower Vistula north of Thorn, became a vassal of the Margrave of Brandenburg, and Danzig fell into German hands for the first time. The Brandenburgers, however, were unable to hold it, and it was not until 1343 that Polish claims to the so-called Pomorze were given up.

Apart from domestic disorders, Poland was also shaken during this period by a disastrous invasion of the Tartars, who in 1241 burned Cracow, invaded Silesia, and sacked Breslau. The depopulation caused both by civil war and this invasion impoverished the Polish princes and induced them to encourage German immigration. The movement had started even before the onslaught of the Tartars, for German villages began to appear in Silesia as early as 1140. But after the Tartar incursion, German settlements spread to every part of Poland. The belt laid waste by the Tartars had been thickly settled since the principal commercial highways between the west and the

Levant passed through Breslau and Cracow. The German settlers therefore followed the line of least resistance and were spared the usual hard pioneer work because the soil they occupied had already been under cultivation for long periods. The colonists received exemption from taxes over a certain fixed term, and could build their towns as they desired, living under their native customs and enjoying absolute home rule.

By the middle of the fourteenth century there were some 150 German village settlements in the modern province of Posen alone, and at the same time cities destroyed by the Tartars were resettled by German colonists, who also founded new towns in Polish territory. Among the rebuilt cities largely populated by Germans in the fourteenth century we may note Sandomierz, Cracow, and Breslau, and among major German settlements at previous Polish centers, Gnesen, Posen, Kalish, Lublin, and even Warsaw itself. As late as 1480, three quarters of the burghers of Warsaw had German names. By the metropolitan cities of Germany these settlements were rightly regarded as outposts of German trade and civilization. The proportion of German population in Poland at the middle of the fourteenth century is estimated at 25 per cent, though many of the German colonists were polonized by the sixteenth. The wave of German settlement extended even beyond Cracow into Eastern Galicia toward Przemysl and Lemberg (Lvóv). Until 1470, indeed, no one but Germans sat on the Lemberg city council.

Simultaneously with the conflict between the Teutonic Order and the Prussians, German conquest and colonization pursued its way up the Baltic seaboard toward the Gulf of Finland. Settlers from Lübeck established themselves for trading purposes at the mouth of the Dvina as early as 1150, but the conquest of Livonia did not begin until the year 1200. Riga was founded as a city and as a missionary bishopric in 1201. The militant Order of the Sword Bearers was then organized to combat the Finnish tribes of the seacoast and the Letts of the interior. They were subject to the Bishop of Riga, and were granted one-third of the land they thus captured. In 1236, however, after a defeat by the Lithuanians, the Sword Bearers combined with the Teutonic Order, and their joint ambitions would have made them masters of the north Russian city-states of Pskov and Novgorod if they had not been defeated by Prince Alexander Nevski on the ice of Lake Peipus in the winter of 1242.

We have dwelt in some detail on these developments to show how remote are all the origins of the political quarrels which have been resumed before our own eyes during the course of the second World War. Yet this extraordinary process was not without its halts and interruptions. Poland recovered much of its driving power under the administration of Kazimir the Great from 1333 to 1370. Meanwhile, the pressure of the Teutonic Order had contributed to unifying Lithuanian resistance, and a strong Lithuania had now developed with a culture predominantly Russian. By 1363, indeed, as we have seen, the Lithuanians had captured Kiev and were advancing toward the Black Sea. The union of Poland and Lithuania, consecrated by the marriage of the Lithuanian Prince Jagailo with Queen Yadwiga of Poland in 1386, was a severe blow to the Teutonic Order, since the conversion of the Lithuanians to Christianity largely deprived the Order of its missionary pretext for existence. The Polish victory at Grünwald-Tannenberg on July 15, 1410 broke its power, and after some further military exchanges a peace of 1422 limited German holdings in East Prussia to frontiers which lasted generally until the Treaty of Versailles.

The activities of the Order in the eastern Baltic continued until the sixteenth century. In Livonia and Esthonia there had been no colonization by German peasants, and the country was thus held only by the nobility, the church, and the citizens. The Muscovite thrust toward the Baltic affected not only the city-states of Pskov and Novgorod, but also the coastal possessions of the Order. The knights successfully resisted Ivan III, but Ivan the Terrible, as we know, took up the task which his grandfather had begun, and as a result of his victories in 1559 the Order was dissolved. Esthonia became Swedish, Livonia fell into Polish hands, and Courland became a hereditary duchy and a fief of the kingdom of Poland. Esthonia and Livonia did not definitely become Russian until the Peace of Nystadt in 1721, and Courland fell into Russian possession only by the third partition of Poland in 1795. Early in the second World War we witnessed the final German surrender of all vested rights in this area acquired since the beginning of the thirteenth century.

Though Poland of the sixteenth century was by no means a peaceful state, it felt the influence of the Protestant reformation and, at least until a Catholic reaction set in under Jesuit direction about 1564 after the Council of Trent, had a reputation for religious tolerance. As a result, the religious wars in Germany started a new current of emigration into Polish territory, especially into the Posen area. At the same time, Low-German Protestants (Mennonites and other reformists) moved into the Pomorze around Danzig, where the local population had been decimated by the thirteen-years' war waged by Kazimir Jagiellonczyk against the weakened Teutonic Order from 1453 to 1466. This Low-German immigration took on greater proportions after Stephen Batory's siege and capture of Danzig in 1577, extending particularly to the courses of the Warthe and Netze rivers. Though the counter-reformation was by this time in full swing throughout Poland, these Protestant settlers, because of their industry and skill in agriculture, were guaranteed religious freedom, and remained free peasants even in an age when serfdom was the native Polish farmer's universal lot. At the same time, however, other settlers came into the lower Vistula valley from Brandenburg and Pomerania under much more onerous conditions, since they were without capital and completely subject to the caprice of their landlords.

This migratory movement was resumed in the seventeenth century during the Thirty Years' War, though many of the refugees from Brandenburg returned from Poland to their homes after the Peace of Westphalia in 1648. In Silesia, however, the persecutions incident to the counter-reformation caused the migration into Poland of some 200,000 Germans, who were responsible for the creation of the textile industry in western Poland. In eastern Poland as well, the German element played a prominent role. In 1648, for instance, when the Cossack Hetman Bogdan Chmelnitski, aided by the Crimean Tartars, threatened eastern Galicia, the German inhabitants of Lemberg paid one third of the ransom by which the city was saved, and German officers and soldiery fought on the Polish side in all the battles of the period.

Sweden came out of the Thirty Years' War greatly strengthened by the momentary possession of the mouths of the Oder, the Elbe, and the Weser, and its king, Charles X, thinking to gain the support of the Elector of Brandenburg for further conquests at Poland's expense, recognized him in 1656 as Duke of Prussia, thereby bringing East Prussia under the sovereignty of Brandenburg. Then, by the Treaty of Wehlau, the next year, the Poles surrendered their claims to East Prussia, thereby assuring the rising Prussian state of the undisputed possession of this area until the Seven Years' War, though it was returned to Prussia after the death of the Empress Elizabeth of Russia in 1762. Silesia was regained by Prussia the next year, the Vistula valley south of Danzig fell to the German share by the first partition of Poland in 1772, and the Posen area followed by the second partition of 1793. Such, then, in its broadest outlines, is the process by which the political frontier between Germany and Poland was determined prior to 1914.

Until the nineteenth century there was little racial hostility between German and Slav. The German expansion eastward during the Middle Ages had been dictated by religious and economic motives, and the conflicts in which Poland, as an independent state, was involved with its neighbors before the partitions were the result of dynastic ambitions and jealousies rather than of any collision of national ideologies. The practical services rendered to the development of agriculture, trade, and industry by German immigrants to Bohemia and Poland require no demonstration. By virtue of its close political association with western Europe, Bohemia was speedily drawn into European intellectual life, and as early as the thirteenth century Bohemian authors were reproducing in their own language the forms and content of German medieval literature. International culture was still more widely disseminated after the foundation of the University of Prague in 1348, and the Hussite movement produced a wave of intellectual activity which lasted until the Thirty Years' War in the seventeenth century.

Poland, because of its comparative remoteness and political instability, was not subject to the same cultural stimuli, and the services rendered by the German settlers in Polish territory were exclusively practical and materialistic. The influence of the Polish crown was never strong enough, nor were its holders cultured enough, to exert a civilizing influence comparable to that which radiated from Prague. Only in the sixteenth century do we meet with a striking development of Polish literature, and here the productive influences were more those of the Renaissance than specifically German, especially since local education was dominated by the Jesuits and strictly limited to the classical curriculum. While German economic influence was strong in both the great western Slavic states, it was Bohemia which profited the most from the absorption of German culture, and it was not until the seventeenth century that political events halted the intellectual advance so auspiciously begun.

Yet it was in Bohemia that the first seeds of a new Slavic racial consciousness sprouted early in the nineteenth century. The age of enlightenment had emphasized the ideals of humanity, tolerance, and culture, and these ideals were spread throughout the Austro-Hungarian monarchy by the reforms of Joseph II. As a matter of fact, the principle of nationality was first formulated by a German, for it was Goethe's great friend and mentor Johann Gottfried Herder, who declared that "the most natural state is a state inhabited by a single nation with a single national character." This principle provoked a grateful echo in the minds of several outstanding Bohemian scholars and patriots. An ex-Jesuit, Joseph Dubrovski, the founder of Slavic philology as a discipline, was the first modern Bohemian patriot of nationalistic stamp, and his works gave to the whole Bohemian literary movement a pan-Slavist direction. He condemned Germanization, but not the Germans, and sincerely believed the Slavs destined to become the bearers of a new civilization. Through Dubrovski, the Czechs began to feel themselves a part of the great Slavic community, and expected to find support for their national aspirations in the new conception of a Slavic civilization.

Contemporary with Dubrovski (who died in 1839) was Joseph Jungmann, translator of *Paradise Lost* and of Châteaubriand's *Atala* who, by his compilation of the first Czech dictionary, revealed the wealth of the mother tongue and by his studies in literary history disclosed the richness and diversity of prior Bohemian literature. Dubrovski's work was carried on by the great antiquarian Paul Joseph Šafařík, a Slovak by birth, whose studies of the origins and expansion of the Slavs constitute a brilliant apologia for the Slavic nations. What Šafařík accomplished in the broad field of philology was duplicated in history by his younger Bohemian colleague, Francis Palacký, and these patriotic and scholarly efforts laid the foundations for a renaissance of Bohemian literature and of general Slavic intellectual life. The first models of the new literature were the products of the romantic movement in German letters, but Bohemian authors soon passed on to independent creation, and it was Joseph Kollár who, animated by his contacts at Jena with the literature of Young Germany, composed eloquent sonnets in which he called the scattered Slavs to solidarity and coöperation in the great work which he, as a disciple of Herder, believed was their destiny. In particular, Kollár preached a community of interests with the South Slavs, a principle which, had it been properly appreciated by the Austrian authorities, might have had incalculable consequences for the maintenance of their Empire.

The ideals preached by Palacký, who was as great a journalist as he was a historian, were first formulated in political terms just prior to the revolutionary year 1848, which signalized the end of Metternich's regime and the dawn of constitutionalism in Austria. It was thus Palacký who advocated an autonomous Bohemia including all the lands which had formerly belonged to the Bohemian crown, together with as much of Hungary as was populated by Slovaks: the principle, indeed, upon which the Czechoslovak state was subsequently erected. It is significant, moreover, that the German elements in Bohemia were inclined to support the Czechs in their agitation for autonomy. But the federal idea was never realized in Austria-Hungary before the monarchy dissolved in 1918, and Bohemian hopes in this direction were dashed by the Austrian Constitution of 1867, which gave the Hungarians a preferred position, as compared with the Slavs, by establishing the principle of dualism, by making Hungary practically autonomous, and by settling the Magyar domination upon Slovaks and Croats. This loss was to some extent offset by educational concessions to the Czechs, since in the previous twenty years Bohemian national consciousness had consolidated to an extraordinary degree through the increased use of the native language and the improved status of both peasants and the middle class. The romantic emphasis laid by Palacký on the glorious past of Bohemia thus proved an altogether healthy spur to the national ambition.

Though after 1867 there was never any real reconciliation between Prague and Vienna, the material prosperity of Bohemia advanced rapidly in the next fifty years, and the part still played by the German element in Bohemia before the war of 1914 is evidenced by the fact that, though they comprised only 37 per cent of the population, they paid 50 per cent of the taxes. But while the Czechs never lost sight of the federalist ideal, this principle was looked on with disfavor by the Viennese autocrats, who felt that any increase in Bohemia's degree of independence would only weaken the whole structure of the unified Austro-Hungarian state. This difference in political philosophy was aggravated by the fact that there was too little will to compromise and too much reverence for history among the Bohemian leaders. Oppressed nations always overestimate the practical importance of past tradition. The dominant position long occupied by the kingdom of Bohemia in the Holy Roman Empire, if the Czechs had only realized it, was of far less moment than any rational compromise which would have permitted Bohemia to enjoy to the full the material advantages it commanded as the most highly industrialized section of Austria-Hungary and, at the same time, to cultivate a national spirit, language and literature, without making itself obnoxious to its neighbors by always harping on the same string. It is, however, an unfortunate truth that the composition, within a state, of quarrels rising from linguistic differences complicated by racial, temperamental, and confessional motives and by the carefully cherished traditions of the past which are, or suppose themselves to be, oppressed, is a problem of baffling complexity. On the other hand, the experience of the twenty years before 1939 definitely showed that this problem is not solved by merely setting up these disaffected areas as national units.

Now while it is true that the Czechs did not find themselves precisely in clover under the Hapsburg monarchy, the fact remains that they achieved a high level of material prosperity and culture during the nineteenth century. They had, to be sure, advanced further along the path of social evolution than the Poles, among whom the middle class had actually contracted when the partitions interrupted the evolution of the nation. When Poland fell there were virtually but two classes in the country, the landowning gentry and the peasants. Serfdom was abolished in the Prussian section in 1821, with a subsequent rapid economic improvement in the peasants' status. After the partitions, the middle class evolved most speedily in the Russian section, and at a slower rate under the German regime. After 1867, the Poles under Austrian sovereignty enjoyed the greatest relative degree of freedom. The local administration passed entirely into Polish hands, the universities of Cracow and Lemberg were Polonized, and Polish was admitted as the official language everywhere except in the military and the postal services. In the Prussian area, the German administration adopted a liberal policy until 1830, when German became the official language, though the local church and the school system remained Polish.

Before 1848, however, pan-Slavic ideals filtered in from Bohemia, and that year saw open revolt in the Posen area. As the middle class grew in numbers, the influence of the nobility waned, and improved educational facilities favored the dissemination of Polish culture and national ideals among the masses. As industry grew in western Germany, there was also a considerable emigration of German residents from the Polish province. German authorities estimate that this movement shifted some three million Germans out of this area during the last half of the nineteenth century. Their places in the cities, which had hitherto been predominantly German, were taken by Polish workers who came in from the country, with the result that the proportion of German population in the Polish cities under German rule declined. At the same time, the general prosperity of Germany benefited the Polish district, the wealth and productivity of which were greatly enhanced during the nineteenth century, and educational opportunities naturally far surpassed those available in either Russian Poland or Galicia.

This survey of relations between German and Slav from the earliest times to the last century demonstrates with reasonable clarity that once the barbarities of the medieval German expansion period were over, every advance in civilization which the Germans experienced was passed on to such of the Western Slavs as were ripe to receive it. Though the Bohemians lost their political independence in the sixteenth century, they had already acquired such a high degree of culture that they were not likely to lag behind the general movement of European civilization. Though not independent, they nevertheless enjoyed a degree of political stability which the Poles lacked. On the other hand, even if the partitions splintered the Polish state, the material and intellectual progress registered under German rule in Posen and under Austrian sovereignty in Galicia also brought the Poles into closer touch with Western Europe and made them participants in the march of progress.

We should not for one moment wish to belittle the Bohemian or the Polish thirst for independent statehood, nor ignore the oppressive measures to which Poles and Czechs alike were frequently subjected by their masters who spoke a different language. But on the record there is no insuperable reason why peaceful coöperation between Slav and German is not possible, and there is no prospect for peace in Europe until this coöperation is reëstablished. Time and the pressure of events will wipe away the official German opinion that the Slavs are an inferior race, just as it has wiped out the brutal German ruling class which holds this opinion. But it is the task of our generation to work out some system whereby political sovereignty is not the ultimate aim of national aspirations, and whereby national units not economically self-sufficient—as none of the Western Slavs are—may join in political associations which guarantee their economic welfare without jeopardizing their characteristic cultures and ideals.

VII

The Balkan Principalities

The Slavs of the Balkan peninsula include the Slovenians, the Croats, the Serbs, and the Bulgarians. It has already been pointed out that the Bulgarians, though Slavic in language, are not pure Slavic racially, since they are the product of the fusion of Turanian invaders with a previous native Slav population. The northernmost of these groups, the Slovenes, are concentrated in Carniola (the territory immediately east of the Italian coastal strip behind Trieste) together with southern Styria as far as the Mur River. They speak a language akin to Serbo-Croatian, but clearly differentiated from it, and number about one and one half millions. Until 1918 their history was identified with that of Austria, and most of their cultural impulses came from colonies of Slovenian emigrants in the United States, especially around Pittsburgh and Cleveland. As a portion of the post-1918 Yugoslav state, they enjoyed linguistic and cultural autonomy with a flourishing Slovenian university at Laibach (Ljubljana). The Croats and the Serbs are one people racially and linguistically, apart from minor dialect differences and the fact that the Croats, being Catholics, use the Latin alphabet, while the Serbs, as members of the Orthodox Church, employ a Cyrillic alphabet closely resembling the Russian. Since the Croats are found in the western part of Bosnia and in Dalmatia, their residence may be roughly defined as a strip running eastward from the Adriatic coast between Fiume and Zara to the Drave river, where they collide with the Magyars, together with a triangular enclave with the middle of its base at Spalato (Split) and its apex just north of Sarajevo.

The Serbs occupy the pre-1914 kingdom of Serbia, northern Macedonia, and the major portion of Bosnia and Herzegovina. The territory inhabited by the Serbs is generally rugged and mountainous. Only at its eastern extremity was it touched by the ancient route from the West to Constantinople, which crossed the Danube at Belgrade, followed the Morava River south to Nish, and then turned eastward into the Bulgarian plain. Geographically, the Serbs were well-protected from foreign invaders, but at the same time internal communication and national union have been hampered until fairly recently by the same factors. That the dividing line between the Eastern and the Western Roman Empires runs straight through the center of Serbian territory (from Lake Skutari to the Drina, and along this river northward to the Save near Sirmium) constitutes a political factor of long-standing importance. The early Serbs had no geographical frontier on the east, and thus blended gradually into the Bulgarians along a line from the junction of the Timok and the Danube southward through Pirot and Kustendil to Macedonia, where the border territory has been hotly contested since the epoch of earliest settlement.

Like their northern kin in Poland and Bohemia, the Balkan Slavs were originally split into minor tribes, headed each by a chief called a *zhupan*. From their first settlement in the Balkans to 1196, the Serbs were at least nominally under the sway of Byzantium. During the height of Bulgarian ascendancy in the ninth and tenth centuries, and again in the thirteenth, considerable portions of eastern Serbia (especially the Morava valley) were also under Bulgarian control. From time to time a more ambitious Serbian chief succeeded in combining several tribes under his sway, but none of these combinations were in any degree permanent. From a geographical standpoint, the country was divided into two main sections, the *pomorje* and

The Balkan Principalities 145

the *zagorje,* that is, seaboard and hinterland. In the ninth century, the advance of the Magyars into Hungary cut off the Serbs from central Europe and the region known as Slavonia, northwest of Belgrade (between Save and Drave), along with Croatia, were absorbed by Hungary in the twelfth century, to remain under Hungarian rule until the end of World War I. In the tenth century the rising power of Venice had also gained control not only of all the islands off the Dalmatian coast but also of the coastal cities.

The first political centers in Serbia rose during the twelfth and the thirteenth centuries: the first in the region of Rashka on the Ibar river, near modern Novipazar, the second in Zeta (modern Montenegro), and the third in Bosnia. The last-named fell first into Byzantine and later into Hungarian hands, so that it never really formed a part of any Serbian state until modern times.

For two hundred years between 1170 and 1371, the principality of Rashka was the dominant Serbian center. Its rise began with the seizure of the principality by an able local prince, Stephen Nemanya, whose efforts at its expansion were favored by the decline of Byzantine prestige after the defeat of the Greek arms by the Seljuq Turks at Myriokephalon, in Asia Minor, in 1176 and especially after the death of the Emperor Manuel Comnenus in 1180. In the next fifty years, the Bulgarian state also degenerated under combined Tartar and Greek pressure, while the Tartar invasions held the Magyars in check. Friendly relations with Venice and commercial exchanges through Ragusa (Dubrovinik) gave the new Serbian principality contacts with Western civilization and some degree of economic prosperity. Stephen Nemanya's domain included the Adriatic seaboard between the Narenta river (west of modern Sarajevo) on the north to the Boyana river (northern boundary of modern Albania) on the south, and extended inland to the Morava river on the east, and southward as far as Prizren. Stephen abdicated in 1196 to enter a monastery at Mount Athos, where his youngest son Savva had already taken holy orders, and together they founded the famous Khilander monastery on the holy mountain.

He was succeeded by his son Stephen Nemanyich (1196-1228), a clever and gifted prince trained in Byzantine culture, a skilful diplomat and a good troop commander, who was the son-in-law of the extremely incompetent Byzantine emperor Alexius Angelus. Since Stephen, though designated for the succession by his father, was junior in the family, he was faced by the revolt of his jealous elder brother, Vukan, and his situation was further jeopardized by Magyar and Bulgarian invasions. The danger was eventually removed by Stephen's still younger brother, the monk Savva, who reconciled his warring brethren. At the fall of Constantinople before the Crusaders in 1204, Stephen put away his Greek wife, the Princess Eudoxia, and later married Anna, granddaughter of the Doge Enrico Dandolo of Venice. Through Venetian intervention he was then able to have himself crowned king by a papal legate in 1217, and was thereafter known in Serbian history as Stephen the First-Crowned. This momentary deviation toward Rome was short-lived, however, since Stephen initiated friendly relations with Theodore Lascaris, the despot of Nicaea, so that his brother Savva was made autocephalous Orthodox archbishop of Serbia in 1219. Savva not only developed a useful activity in the organization and expansion of the Serbian church, but also distinguished himself as an author of monastic rules and of a short biography of his father: his royal brother Stephen also wrote on the same subject, so that these two princes are actually the first native Serbian authors.

Before his death in 1228, Stephen designated his son Radoslav as his successor, but the latter proved a weak and ineffective ruler. After the Latin seizure of Constantinople in 1204, Michael Angelus had become the ruler of Epirus. His brother and successor, Theodore Angelus, after capturing Salonika in 1222 and thus extending his realm from the Adriatic to the Aegean, had himself crowned Emperor of the Greeks. As early as 1216, Stephen had sought to marry Radoslav to Angelus's

The Balkan Principalities

daughter Anna, but the Greek clergy had objected. But now that Theodore had climbed higher, this objection was abandoned and the marriage took place. In consequence, Radoslav as king of Serbia was entirely under the thumb of his ambitious father-in-law, but Theodore's power was destroyed in 1230 through his disastrous defeat by the Bulgarians, who thereupon drove Radoslav out of Serbia in 1234 and set his brother Vladislav on the throne.

Vladislav's reign is remarkable for the invasion of the Tartars who, after devastating southern Russia, destroyed Cracow and Breslau, defeated the Magyars, and in 1241 penetrated even to the Adriatic coast where, though unable to reduce the fortress of Spalato (Split), they ravaged as far south as Antivari, in Montenegro. Though the Serbs suffered comparatively little, because they hid themselves in mountain and forest fastnesses, yet by the time the Tartars withdrew in 1242, Vladislav's whole realm was disorganized to the point where little remained of it save the coastal districts. This remnant he therefore resigned in 1243 to his younger brother Stephen Urosh I, and the next eighty years were enlivened by a series of recurrent conflicts with Hungary, Bulgaria, and Byzantium. This period was marked nevertheless by a considerable economic advance because of the wealth derived from the renewed exploitation of the old Roman gold and silver mines, which provided the means for building up a strong military force aimed at the Byzantine Palaeologi.

The high point of medieval Serbian history was reached during the reign of Stephen Urosh's great-grandson Stephen Dushan, who served as junior regent under his father from 1321 until ten years later he deposed the latter and became king in his own name. Dushan's court at Skoplje included Serbs, Bulgarians (for his mother was Bulgarian), Greeks, Albanians, Saxons from the mining towns, German knights, and merchants from Venice and Florence. It thus possessed a marked international character. Apart from his campaigns, Dushan concerned himself with laws, with the introduction of an orderly administrative and judicial system, and with the protection of trade routes. Friendly relations were maintained with Ragusa. Unfortunately, like many other early Slavic rulers elsewhere, he was unable to curb the overwhelming influence of the nobility. The sudden expansion of Serbian territory during his reign led to the acquisition of excessive power by the various district governors, and since his successor proved to be a youth without talent or capacity, the kingdom rapidly transformed itself into an unstable oligarchy. Dushan's rapid acquisition of Macedonia, Albania, Epirus, and Thessaly was facilitated by disordered conditions in the Byzantine Empire, and carried through without one major military operation. He neglected his northern frontier, however, which was not always secure against the Hungarians, nor could the Bosnians be driven from the coast above Ragusa. Dushan remained on good terms with Venice and also with Bulgaria, in the latter instance thanks largely to family connections.

Dushan's gains to the south were made possible by the fourteen years of civil war which followed the death of the Byzantine emperor Andronicus III in 1341, and the ease with which these conquests were accomplished led him logically to the hope of seizing the whole empire, even the metropolis of Constantinople itself. As one Byzantine commentator remarked, "The great Serb, like an overflowing river that has passed far beyond its banks, has already submerged one part of the empire of Romania with its waves, and is threatening to engulf another." He betrothed his young son in 1343 to the sister of the Emperor John V Palaeologus. In 1346, with the consent of the Serbian parliament of nobles (*drzhavni sabor*), he proclaimed himself "Tsar of the Serbs and the Greeks," and upon notifying the Venetians of his impending coronation "in imperio constantinopolitano," he offered them an alliance for the overthrow of the empire, which the Venetians declined with thanks. According to Byzantine notions, an emperor should be supported by a patriarch. So Dushan, without the consent of the Byzantine hierarchy but with the willing support of the

The Balkan Principalities 149

Bulgarian and Serbian prelates who were dependent on his favor, named his own Serbian archbishop as "patriarch of the Serbs and the Greeks," and then had himself crowned as emperor by this patriarch at Skoplje on Easter Day, 1346. He proceeded to organize his court on the Byzantine basis, and in 1349 promulgated his own law code, or *Zakonnik*.

Dushan's last years were disturbed by constant war with the Bosnians on the seacoast, and in October 1350, while he was on a campaign against them, news suddenly arrived that the Greeks had taken the offensive in Macedonia and captured Salonika. The situation was complicated not only by the coexistence of two competing Byzantine emperors but also by the menacing presence of the Ottoman Turks across the Bosporus. While Dushan might have captured Byzantium in the absence of the Turks, they too were aiming at the metropolis, and his troops were not capable of withstanding their well-marshaled forces. Recognizing the danger inherent in the first Turkish settlement on the European side at Gallipoli in 1353, Dushan the next year sent an embassy to Pope Innocent VI at Avignon, by which he offered to join the Roman Church if the latter would designate him as supreme commander against the Turks. The Pope was favorable to this proposal, which was also approved by Charles IV of Bohemia. Unfortunately, however, King Louis of Hungary chose this moment to invade northern Serbia, and a new turn of events eliminated one of the contending emperors at Constantinople. The papal envoy was thus coolly received at the Serbian court, and departed in a huff for Hungary to urge the Magyars to speed up their operations against Dushan. The Venetians, disturbed by the possibility of a Hungarian threat to the Dalmatian coast, were negotiating with the Serbs for the purchase of certain coastal towns when Dushan himself died on December 20, 1355, at the age of forty-eight years.

The existence of Dushan's monarchy was of such short duration that in its history little is to be observed save its formation and its disintegration. Ten years after Dushan's death his empire seemed something of the remote past. We are, however, somewhat better informed about the social and political consistency of the Serbian state in Dushan's day than in later periods. In the fourteenth century Serbia did not differ very essentially from the western nations of the same age, since its king was dependent on the estates, while nobility and clergy formed the ruling caste, and exploitation of the peasantry was becoming more intense. Though many princes of the house of Nemanya were gifted, they were not surrounded by nobility of equal attainments. The Serbian magnates had no understanding of the need for a strong central authority, with the result that their selfishness and rising influence brought the Serbian state to collapse far earlier than was the case in Poland. The king had no fixed capital, but moved from one castle to another according to seasons or political developments. He was surrounded by a council of prominent dignitaries, while the old Serbian diets, which usually were convened by royal command in royal castles at high festivals, were composed of officials, major and minor nobility, and church dignitaries.

The Serbian hereditary military nobility developed only from the tenth century, while a higher nobility made up of members of the royal family, chiefs of clans, and royal officials did not appear till two centuries later. In practice all arms-bearing free commoners belonged to the lower nobility, while the peasants bore the characteristic name of *sebri,* meaning tenants or mortgagors. The country population exclusive of the nobles was split into two classes, the farming peasantry, which gradually became more attached to the soil, and the much freer shepherds. Small farms rather than large estates were the rule. The shepherds were for the most part immigrant Vlakhs (that is, Danubian Romans who had come into the country since the fifth century under the pressure of nomadic movements) and Amarets or Albanians.

The establishment of a national church dates from the consecration of Savva as archbishop of Serbia in 1219, and its traditional nucleus was at Peć (Ipek), about forty miles south of modern Novipazar. The Roman Church was strong only along the coast, with a bishopric at Antivari, though most of the Nemanyich princes maintained friendly relations with the curia. The cities of Serbia were partly old communities of Roman or Greek origin and partly new centers formed since the thirteenth century at trading posts and mines, though these newer towns never reached the stage of development attained by many urban communities set up in Croatia and Hungary after the Tartar incursion. The Romanic municipalities on the coast, with definite fixed boundaries, enjoyed considerable autonomy. They were ruled by general assemblies which gradually transformed themselves into aristocratic councils. They possessed their own law codes, and elected new judges every year. In each such city the king of Serbia had a representative known as a *comes* or *knez*. The native cities of inland Serbia were mainly unfortified market places in the vicinity of some fortified stronghold to which the inhabitants might withdraw in time of danger.

Compared with neighboring areas (for instance, Bulgaria, periodically disturbed by incursions of nomads from the south Russian steppes, or the declining Byzantine Empire), Serbia, especially from 1282 to 1355, may be classed as a rich country. The national wealth, mostly in the hands of the king, the nobility, and the clergy, consisted primarily of cattle. Agriculture suffered from labor shortage. Placer gold mines were operated near Novipazar and Prizren, while silver was found in Bosnia. Judged by modern standards, these mineral deposits were scanty, but the high value of precious metals before the discovery of America made extraction worth while.

Upon the death of Stephen Dushan, his conquests rapidly melted away because none of his successors possessed the energy or the prestige to hold the country together. By 1358, the Hungarians were in possession of the whole Dalmatian coast as far as Ragusa, while the Greeks recovered Epirus and Thessaly. The Turks continued to spread through Thrace, and in 1371 laid the foundation for their future domination of the South

Slavs by defeating at the Maritza river a Serbian force moving to attack the Turks at Adrianople, which had been in Turkish hands for the preceding ten years. Turkish cavalry raiders now harried Macedonia as far as Thessaly and Albania. The local Slavic princes were reduced to the status of tributaries one by one, till the Pope even consulted with the King of Hungary and the Doge of Venice as to means of meeting the impending danger. From 1371, Serbia was no longer a unified kingdom, but an agglomeration of districts held by individual nobles, while the title of king was in dispute. Only to the extreme north, along the Danube and Save between the Morava and the Drina rivers did one small and well-ordered district survive. By 1386, the Turks had conquered Nish, broken into Bosnia (which had heretofore been a feudatory of Hungary), and even pushed into the Narenta valley of Sarajevo.

In 1388, the defeat of a Turkish force in Bosnia inspired the Sultan Murad to undertake a major campaign against Serbia and the Adriatic coast. Serbs, Croats, and Bosnians united for resistance, and met the Turks in a disastrous battle fought at *Kossovo Polje* (Magpie's Field) north of Skoplje, on St. Vitus's Day (*Vidov dan*), June 15, 1389. A Serbian noble suspected of treachery proved his courage that day by entering the Turkish camp as a deserter and assassinating Murad in his tent. His son Bayazid was immediately proclaimed emir in his stead and won the battle, but was obliged to retire to Adrianople to consolidate his forces. When the Turks thus withdrew, the news was sent out to Italy and to western Europe that the Christians had gained the victory. Such was not the case, however, for this fatal struggle broke the resistance of the peoples in the northwestern section of the Balkans and founded the Osmanic hegemony which was to endure in this area for five hundred years.

The Turkish menace hung heavy over the Serbian people for the next century, and this situation was rendered more serious by the constant Hungarian threat from the north. The pressure was momentarily relieved in 1402 through Bayazid's

The Balkan Principalities 153

defeat by Tamerlane, and Stephen Lazarevich, the energetic prince of northern Serbia, threw off the Turkish yoke to become a vassal of Hungary. The respite was short-lived, however, and by 1428 Stephen's nephew and successor George Brankovich, after losing his hold on Nish and the valley of the middle Morava, was obliged to accept Turkish sovereignty once more.

The middle years of the fifteenth century are replete with joint Hungarian and Serbian efforts to drive back the Turks, sometimes with temporary success, but more often without positive results. After a brief breathing spell in 1451, Mohammed II made his culminating attack on Constantinople, which was captured on May 29, 1453. Without waiting for the expiration of the existing truce with Hungary and Serbia, Mohammed reopened hostilities. His first campaign netted 50,000 enslaved Serbian prisoners, the devastation of the entire country, and a Turkish advance to the gates of Semendria, the stronghold built by George Brankovich on the Danube at the mouth of the Morava. After a successful retaliatory raid southward by Hungarian forces, the Turks returned to the assault in 1455, but were defeated and repulsed before Belgrade the next year. Unfortunately the ensuing deaths of the able Hungarian commander John Hunyadi and of Brankovich himself, both of whom had been the guiding spirits of resistance to the Turks, paralyzed further efforts to protect Serbia, and with the fall of Semendria in June 1459 the history of the old Serbian state came to a close.

Bosnia, which had hitherto suffered only from sporadic raids, now became the goal of attack. Prior to 1377, the Bosnian princes had been vassals of Hungary, but one of them then profited from Hungarian complications with Poland to declare himself independent. Herzegovina split off from Bosnia only in 1448. But the Turks invaded Bosnia in 1463, when they captured and slew the last local king, and after that their conquest of the country was complete and rapid. A great exodus of Slavic population ensued, but numerous landowners adopted Islam to retain their possessions, a fact which explains the relatively large number of Slavic Mohammedans in Bosnia to the present day. Twenty years later Herzegovina met the same fate, while Zeta (modern Montenegro) held out until 1496. At the end of the fifteenth century, the Turks were masters of all the Serbian districts except Croatia and Slavonia, which belonged to Hungary, and the Dalmatian coastline, which was divided between Hungary and Venice. The only center in which medieval Serbian culture survived was Ragusa (Dubrovnik), and the decline of the Turks, signalized by rapid Austrian reconquest in Serbia, Bosnia, and Romania, began only with the victory of Don Juan of Austria at Lepanto in 1571.

We have seen that Christianity was introduced into Bulgaria in 865 by the conversion of Prince Boris, who subsequently gave shelter to numerous disciples of Constantine and Methodius after their flight from Moravia. At the beginning of the tenth century, under the rule of Simeon the Great, younger son of Boris, Bulgaria attained a high degree of power and prosperity, including most of the Balkan peninsula south of the Danube and east of the Serbian rivers Morava, Ibar, and Drina. Simeon plays somewhat the same role in Bulgarian history that Stephen Dushan does in the Serbian annals. He too wished to conquer Byzantium, and in 917 he advanced his banners almost to the gates of Constantinople, but was diverted from his purpose by a Serbian revolt inspired by Byzantine diplomacy. After seven years of intermittent warfare, a precarious peace was negotiated in 925, and two years later, after involving himself in a disastrous Serbian campaign, in which his troops were soundly defeated, Simeon passed to his reward.

During Simeon's reign, Bulgaria made significant progress in culture and wealth, and the Macedonian school at Okhrida founded by Clement, Methodius's disciple, developed a number of competent scholars who translated and adapted works of Greek ecclesiastical literature. This labor was continued and expanded by the school founded by Simeon himself at his new

The Balkan Principalities

capital, Preslav, on the little river Tutsa, some sixty miles from the port of Varna. Here Simeon endeavored to found another Constantinople, and adorned the city with ostentatious splendor. The country profited by sales of grain and cattle to the Greek Empire. Its coastal roads also carried merchandise to and from the steppe country of Russia, while the main route from central Europe to Constantinople entered the Balkans at Belgrade, followed the Morava river down to Nish, and there divided, the western branch running down the Vardar to Salonika, while the eastern fork touched Sardica (now Sofia), and went on to Philippopolis (Plovdiv), Adrianople, and Constantinople. Simeon did not hesitate to undertake military reprisals against the Greeks when the commercial interests of his subjects were interfered with.

Upon Simeon's death, however, his realm disintegrated as fast as Stephen Dushan's was to melt away in the fourteenth century. His successors proved incompetent, and were menaced by rebellious princes, first in Serbia, then in Macedonia. After 963 the whole western section became independent, and the eastern half was to all intents and purposes a Greek protectorate. The authority of the Bulgarian princes was also undermined by the rapid spread of the picturesque Bogomile heresy, whose adherents refused submission to either church or state and resisted both taxation and military service. They were frankly dualist, contrasting God with Satan, good with evil, light with darkness, spirit with matter, and considering both forces equal. The progress of civilization in Bulgaria came to a standstill. We have, for example, the description of a Bulgarian envoy who appeared at the Byzantine court in 968 quite unwashed, with his head shaved, and wearing a brass belt to keep his trousers up.

Meanwhile, the Byzantine Empire was gaining in strength with the military prowess of Nicephorus Phocas, the conqueror of the Saracens. An ill-judged Bulgarian demand for tribute in 965 provoked an immediate hostile response. Nicephorus not only invaded Bulgaria, but bribed Sviatoslav, Prince of

Kiev and father of Vladimir I, to overrun the country. For the next four years Sviatoslav was master of Bulgaria and thought of settling there permanently. In fact, he began to cherish designs on Constantinople itself. Nicephorus had been murdered in 969, and the Byzantine throne was now occupied by the energetic and unscrupulous John Tzimisces, who was not disposed to tolerate Sviatoslav's pretensions. In the spring of 971 he thus drove the Russians out of Preslav, and defeated Sviatoslav at Silistria, on the lower Danube.

The defeated Russian agreed to return to Kiev, but before taking ship, he requested the privilege of an interview with his victorious adversary. John Tzimisces rode down to the Danube panoplied in golden armor and escorted by numerous horsemen equipped with equal splendor. The Prince of Kiev approached in a little boat, rowing with the other oarsmen. He was of robust build and moderate stature, with bristling brows, blue eyes, and a flat nose. His beard was sparse, and he wore long mustaches. His head was shorn save for two long braids at either side, which designated his high station. In one ear he wore an earring set with two pearls and a carbuncle between them. In dress he was undistinguishable from his fellows, except that his white tunic was cleaner than theirs. Having thus confronted the incarnation of Byzantine glory, Sviatoslav set out for the capital which he had deliberately abandoned and was never more to see, for he was slain the next spring on his homeward journey by the nomad Pechenegs near the site of the modern Dneprostroi dam.

After eastern Bulgaria was thus subjected to Byzantium, the national spirit lived on only in Macedonia. By 973, a local prince named Samuel was establishing his supremacy, and Bulgarian envoys appeared at the court of the German emperor Otto I. After 976, when John Tzimisces died and his young successors were involved in the civil wars which subsequently gave Vladimir I of Kiev a chance to marry the Princess Anna and become converted, Samuel profited by these diversions to extend his sway southward into Thessaly and eastward

The Balkan Principalities 157

into Thrace. In 986, a Byzantine punitive expedition was overthrown, and Samuel's realm grew through Bulgaria to the coast of the Black Sea. He had thus restored the empire of Simeon the Great. In 985 he captured Berrhoea, west of Salonika, and in 989 Philip of Macedon's old capital at Larissa in Thessaly, which he held for seven years. Despite the recovery of Larissa by the Greeks in 996, Samuel concentrated his attention on the Adriatic coast while the Emperor Basil II was engrossed with hostilities against the Saracens in Syria. But Basil returned to the charge in 1001, and in four years Samuel lost the entire eastern half of his realm. Successive defeats soon decimated his forces, and in the autumn of 1014 he died. Basil's repeated campaigns continued until 1019, when the whole of Bulgaria was subjected to Byzantine authority.

Of the internal history of Samuel's reign we know next to nothing beyond the fact that taxes were paid in kind, and that this Macedonian prince, though a great builder of fortresses and churches, did not share the concern for learning which had characterized Simeon before him. The nation was, in fact, totally lacking in cohesion and organization, and thus owed its offensive power purely to the energy of a gifted leader. Once he was taken from the scene, the centrifugal tendencies of the feudal nobles won the day.

The last upsurge of medieval Bulgarian nationalism took place late in the twelfth century. Byzantium was by that time frankly decadent as the feudal power of the great provincial landlords increased, to the manifest detriment of imperial authority, while the empire had been weakened by disastrous wars with the Seljuq Turks in Asia Minor, complicated by friction with the Western crusading states. In 1186, one year after the accession of Isaac Angelus, a spendthrift and a cruel nonentity, Bulgarian dissatisfaction with Byzantine rule provoked a revolt in eastern Bulgaria which centered at Tirnovo. It was headed by John and Peter Asen, two members of the old Bulgarian nobility, who had grown up among the Vlakhs, or Romanians, and the latter also participated actively in the insurrection. This movement coincided exactly with the rise of Rashka in Serbia under Stephen Nemanya, who allied himself with Peter Asen. The allies endeavored to secure the favorable ear of Frederick Barbarossa, who in 1189 passed through the Balkans on the Third Crusade, but without obtaining any binding assurance. Even so, the Bulgarians inflicted a crushing defeat on Isaac Angelus, and in 1195 he was deposed by his brother Alexius, the father-in-law of the Serbian prince Stephen Nemanyich, the First-Crowned. A year later both John and Peter Asen were murdered as a result of Byzantine intrigues, but their policy was continued by their young brother Kaloyan.

During the struggle between Stephen Nemanyich and his brother Vukan for the Serbian throne, Kaloyan had seized Nish and held all eastern Serbia from the Danube south to Skoplje. His position in this area was threatened by the Magyars, but Kaloyan, who had been brought up in Constantinople, had some notions of diplomacy. He accordingly opened negotiations with Pope Innocent III, with the result that a papal legate crowned him as king of the Bulgarians and the Vlakhs late in 1204. The Crusaders, who had just taken Constantinople, then endeavored to establish their sovereignty over Kaloyan, who rejected the notion flatly, and after allying himself with the nomad Polovtsi or Kumans north of the Danube (it may be recalled that their kin in the steppe country were the chief source of worry at Kiev during the twelfth century), undertook numerous raids into Byzantine territory. Baldwin I, the Latin Emperor of Byzantium, led a punitive expedition against Kaloyan, but was defeated and murdered. Then, after further success, Kaloyan himself was murdered while preparing to attack Salonika in 1207.

Ten years of anarchy ensued before Kaloyan's son John Asen II firmly established himself on the Bulgarian throne in 1218. One of his daughters married Vladislav of Serbia, son of Stephen the First-Crowned, and another was married to Manuel, the brother of Theodore Angelus, despot of Epirus, since 1223 emperor at Salonika. Asen himself, though not a conqueror, was talented and educated, and he expanded the boundaries of the kingdom, which he had received in a disorganized state, to limits it had not reached in several centuries and never achieved afterward. Tolerant in religious matters and clement, he left a good name not only among the Bulgarians but among the Greeks as well. In fact, when Robert de Courtenay, Latin Emperor of Byzantium, died in 1228, Asen was seriously thought of as possible regent for his eleven-year-old son Baldwin, but the project collapsed before the opposition of the Latin knights and clergy.

Asen had been allied up to this point with Theodore Angelus, the Greek emperor at Salonika. On hearing of the regency proposal, Theodore, who himself had natural designs on Constantinople, became jealous of Asen and opened hostilities. Asen's defeat of Theodore in 1230 broke the power of the empire at Salonika and at one stroke made Asen master of Thrace to Adrianople, of Macedonia, and of Albania, while through his son-in-law Vladislav he was factually the sovereign of Serbia as well. Allied with John Vatatses of Nicaea and Manuel Angelus of Salonika, Asen in 1235 coöperated in an attack on Constantinople, but he soon saw the danger for himself in any reunion of the rival Greek factions which might rehabilitate their sovereignty at Constantinople, and again became a defender of the Latin Empire. He thus joined Baldwin II in a campaign against the Greeks in Thrace in 1239, which he suddenly abandoned on receiving the news of the death of his wife and son from the plague at Tirnovo, and then died himself in 1241.

Asen's successors dropped his pro-Latin policy to ally themselves with the able despot of Nicaea, John Vatatzes, the chief Greek pretender to the Byzantine throne, who extended his possessions on the mainland at the expense of Asen's weaker heirs, and by 1257 the Asen dynasty was extinct. The nobles then chose as king a grandson of Stephen Nemanya, the Serbian Prince Constantine, who was hard-pressed by Hungarian invaders. Involved by his Greek wife in Byzantine politics (for the Latin Empire had fallen in 1261 and Michael Palaeologus was now emperor), he secured the aid of the Tartars (who were by this time established in Russia and eagerly seized an excuse to devastate Thrace), but was later murdered by an ambitious commoner. Under Constantine's heirs a series of pretenders, intrigues, and Tartar invasions paralyzed the Bulgarian state, and it fell easily into the hands of Stephen Dushan's father in 1330. A year later Stephen Dushan usurped the Serbian throne, and strengthened his position by marrying a Bulgarian princess whose brother served as regent of Bulgaria.

In 1356, one year after Dushan's death, the Turks crossed the Hellespont. Ten years later, Adrianople was already the capital of Sultan Murad. In 1389, the sultan forced John Shishman, the last tsar of Bulgaria, to become his vassal, and the next June came the disaster at *Kossovo Polje*. Bulgaria was again attacked in 1393. Tirnovo was destroyed, and the patriarch of the Bulgarian church barely managed to exchange death for exile, so that Bulgarian Christians fell under the control of the patriarch of Okhrida. John Shishman was killed by the Sultan Bayazid in 1395.

The Turkish domination over Bulgaria lasted for four hundred eighty-four years, from 1393 to 1878. Because of its geographical configuration and accessibility, Bulgaria was more rapidly and more completely reduced to subjection than Serbia, and it was slower to emancipate itself. National life and aspirations were at a standstill. Those who wished to live peaceably under Turkish rule could do so only as serfs or as Moslems; anyone resisting this choice had no alternative except to become an outlaw in the mountainous districts. On the other hand, the Turkish regime was no more brutal than the various native rulers had been during the period of disorder which had ensued after the death of John Asen II. Yet it was oppressive, and it provoked resistance and revolt for the repression of which the Turks used violent and cruel means.

The Balkan Principalities

Their religious tolerance was greater at the height of their power than during their decline when the central authority grew weaker and the authority passed into the hands of despotic governors. The situation was also complicated by the Greek control of the Bulgarian church. This control was vested in the Greco-Bulgarian patriarchate of Okhrida, in Macedonia, from 1393 to 1767. Positions in this hierarchy were purchased from the Turkish authorities at high prices which could be met only by those Greeks who had made money as officials of the Turkish bureaucracy. Hence the Bulgarian Christians were spiritually governed from Stambul (Constantinople). The independent patriarchates were abolished in 1767, and Greek dominance thus became absolute. The Greek hierarchy made every conceivable effort to wipe out the last vestiges of Bulgarian national spirit in the church, thus arousing among the Bulgarians a bitter hatred which lasted well down into modern times.

The lot of the Serbs under Turkish dominion was, if anything, lighter than the situation under which their Bulgarian kindred labored. Apart from being more remote, Serbian territory was precipitous and irregular, so that conquest and supervision were more difficult. The very fact that Serbian nationality was split between various nuclei, like Serbia proper, Bosnia, Herzegovina, and Montenegro, was doubtless a bar to unity, but this parcellation, though a handicap to political union, guaranteed that the national consciousness would not be easily extinguished. Many Serbs also migrated to neighboring countries not under Turkish rule, especially where other closely related Slavs resided, for a Catholic Croat was infinitely preferable to the infidel as a neighbor or a master. Dalmatia, Slavonia (between Drave and Save), and the so-called Banat in Hungary north of Belgrade, were the chief destinations of this movement, which began even before the fall of Semendria in 1459 and, as the Turks drove farther north, the Serbian settlements extended still more deeply into Hungary. These border districts in Hungary and Croatia were organized by the Austrians as a military buffer against the Turks, and the immigrants received special privileges. A similar situation prevailed in Dalmatia, where the Serbs performed the same function for Venice. One unfortunate result of this migration was the almost complete depopulation of southern Serbia, which was resettled by Albanian mountaineers, while the intellectuals moved to Russia or to Walachia and Moldavia. The strong Slavic influence on Romanian culture dates from this period. Ragusa, though tributary to the Turks, remained a wealthy commercial city and was the only center of Serbian literature during the Middle Ages.

After the fall of Semendria in 1459, the old Serbian patriarchate of Peć (Ipek) was abolished, and the Serbs, like the Bulgarians, were subjected to the patriarchate of Okhrida. This situation lasted, however, only until 1557, when it happened that a high Turkish official of Serbian origin resurrected the patriarchate of Peć for his brother, a Serbian monk who had not adopted Islam. This patriarchate controlled not only the Orthodox Church in Bosnia and the neighboring districts, but was even set by the Turks to supervise resident Catholics. Peć was abolished in 1767 along with Okhrida, however, and the Serbian Christians suffered the same Phanariote Greek oppression as their Bulgarian brethren. Serbian resentment against the Greek clergy ran so high that conversions to Islam became frequent. Though the Slavic liturgy did live on in the remote Bulgarian villages, Serbia had until the nineteenth century only Greek bishops who knew very little Serbian or Church Slavic, and it was on the whole a fortunate circumstance that by this time Greek culture had sunk to so low a level as to be incapable of exerting any attraction on the South Slavic populations exposed to the influence of the Greek clergy. The whole situation of the Orthodox Slavs under Turkish and Greek tutelage explains why religion does not play the same role among Serbians and Bulgarians as it did among the Russian masses prior to the present century.

Because of their long Turkish subjection, all these events of the late Middle Ages are much closer to the Balkan Slavs than to nations which have enjoyed longer periods of independence. Had these Slavs ever achieved an enduring sense of unity, their resistance to Turkish conquest would have been more resolute and effective.

VIII

Servitude and Liberation

During the Turkish supremacy from 1496 when Montenegro was as last subjected to 1796 when the Montenegrins drove the Turks back to Skutari and were thus the first South Slavic state to win virtual independence, the very dispersion of Serbian national life which had been a weakness under the old kingdom made it difficult for the Turks to wipe out the Serbian spirit of independence, which was also fostered in the emigrant communities where Serbs lived exempt from the Turkish yoke.

The prime of the Ottoman Empire was reached early in the sixteenth century. The battle of Lepanto, won by Don Juan of Austria in 1571, was the first portent of its decline. Yet it was not until a century later, after the repulse of the Turks before Vienna in 1683, that a great occidental reaction against the Ottoman menace developed. The Austrians took the offensive, and in 1689, by the Treaty of Karlovcy, at Turkish expense extended their possessions in southern Hungary as far as the river Theiss, northeast of Belgrade. Then, in 1717, Prince Eugene of Savoy regained Slavonia, between the Danube and the Save, and the Turks not only abandoned a portion of Bosnia but also retired south of the Danube, while Dalmatia was returned to Venetian control. Unfortunately, however, this gain was only temporary, since the unsuccessful campaign of 1737-1739, which was accompanied by a Serbian uprising, resulted in an Austrian withdrawal north of the Danube, followed by cruel Turkish reprisals against the rebellious Serbs.

While the Austrians up to this time had regarded their Serbian colonists as a military asset, about the middle of the eighteenth century their attitude was reversed. Since the Empress Maria Theresa (1740-1780) was favorably disposed to the Hungarians, her reign witnessed systematic persecution of the Orthodox Serbs resident in Hungary to whom pressure was applied for the purpose of turning them to Catholicism. As a result, a considerable number emigrated to southern Russia. The situation was relieved during the short reign of Joseph II (1780-1790), who allied himself with Catherine II to drive the Turks out of Europe. Serbian volunteers composed about one-sixth of the Austrian troops in the resulting operations, and a Serbian uprising took place in the lower Morava valley. But when Leopold II came to the throne in 1790, Austrian fortunes turned for the worse, and in 1791 the treaty of Svishtovo gave back the whole of Serbia to the Turks, though some Turkish garrisons were withdrawn. Conditions in Serbian territory were thus, for the moment, somewhat improved, especially in consequence of increased trade with Austria. This development was, however, halted by the disintegration of Turkish authority, which was no longer able to maintain discipline in its frontier provinces. Strife between rival pashas (local governors) thus became the rule, and the atrocities of the janissaries were resumed.

The tyranny of the semi-independent pashas and their minions eventually stirred the quiescent Serbs to revolt, not so much against the sultan as against their local oppressors. Indeed, certain loyal Turks even encouraged the Serbian rebellion. The leaders of the rebels were, in the main, men who had acquired some property, especially in cattle trade, and were therefore concerned about the instability prevailing under Turkish rule. In February, 1804, the rebels chose as their leader Karageorge or Black George Petrovich, from Topola in Shumadiya (northern Serbia), who had had military experience as a guerrilla fighter and as a noncommissioned officer in the Austrian volunteer service—illiterate, but clever and active for his fifty years. Among the prime movers stood various prominent members of the Serbian clergy, while numerous Serbs in the Austrian military service joined the uprising, and prosperous Serbs resident on Austrian soil contributed money and equipment. At the same time, contacts with racial kin in Bosnia, Herzegovina, and Montenegro gave the movement a general character. The Austrians offered no assistance to the Serbs, but the Russian Tsar Alexander I, despite his contemporaneous conflict with Napoleon, supplied both money and moral support.

By 1807, practically unaided, the rebels cleared the Turks from northern Serbia and gained possession of Belgrade and other cities along the northern frontier. The Russians then took the field on the lower Danube, but after some successes hostilities were halted, and the resulting lull was enlivened by dissensions among the Serbian leaders, who were ready to fight one another if no common foe was available. The new state was at first simply a free union of independent districts, and the local chiefs recognized Karageorge only as their military leader. Upon a Russian suggestion, however, a small council of state had also been set up in 1805 with combined judicial and legislative functions. There likewise existed an assembly, or *skupshtina,* composed of district commanders and chiefs, which voted taxes and military levies and controlled public expenditures. Such a *skupshtina* elected Karageorge chief of state in 1808, at which time he recognized the council of state as a supreme court and as an executive body.

When the Russians once more resumed hostilities with the Turks in 1809, the Serbs coöperated by invading Bosnia and at the same time starting two southward offensives, one toward Novipazar and the other toward Nish, with the idea of cutting the Turks off from the west. A junction was also successfully effected with the Montenegrins. The Serbs registered some successes in Bosnia and old Serbia, while the Russians operated largely on Bulgarian soil, and under Kutuzov's command seriously defeated the Turks at Rustchuck (on the Danube) in 1811. But early in 1812 Napoleon allied himself with Prussia and Austria against Russia, which hastily concluded the Peace of Bucharest with the Turks. This treaty provided that the sultan should thereafter deal with the Serbs as an autonomous tributary, but that the conditions of peace between Serbs and Turks should be directly negotiated between the interested parties. The Serbs protested at this Russian policy, but the Russians pointed out that with Napoleon marching on Moscow they had lost control of the situation. Knowing this, the Turks stalled off negotiations for six months until the Russian troops had been withdrawn, and then indicated that the only possible conditions of peace would be a return to the status quo before the uprising of 1804, that is, that the Serbs should give up everything they had won in the previous seven years. When the Serbs rejected these terms, the Turks invaded Serbia from three points, and by September 1813, they were once more masters of Serbia, while Karageorge fled across the Danube into Austria. Before the subjection of Serbia, Napoleon had in 1805 secured all previous Venetian possessions on the eastern Adriatic coast down to the Bocche di Cattaro, together with Carinthia and Croatia south of the Save River, but the Congress of Vienna of 1815 returned this territory to Austria.

After the recapture of Serbia, the Turkish rule was more onerous and cruel than ever before. The first reaction against it began in the fall of 1814, but was brutally suppressed. As a result of Turkish barbarities, a secret meeting of Serbian patriots the next year initiated a second rebellion, the leadership of which they entrusted to Milosh Obrenovich, equal to Karageorge in bravery and energy, but his superior in self-control and diplomacy. The uprising began during Holy Week. When the Turks prepared to take revenge for its initial successes, they were deterred by a threat of Russian intervention, so that a peace was negotiated in 1815 on the basis of the autonomy of northern Serbia under a pasha resident in Belgrade. The *skupshtina* of 1817 then elected Milosh as hereditary prince of Serbia, which he was to rule as the sultan's viceroy.

Though Milosh made some progress toward restoring domestic order in a region where conditions were chaotic and crimes of violence appallingly frequent, he still had difficulty in regulating his relations with the sultan, for the Peace of 1815 had never been ratified and the Turks refused to recognize his status as hereditary prince. Not until 1826 was a satisfactory solution reached, when Nicholas I of Russia brought pressure to bear on the Turks toward an accurate execution of the Treaty of Bucharest at a moment when the Turks were occupied with war in Greece and threatened by a revolt of the janissaries in Stambul itself. The result was the Convention of Akerman (near Odessa), whereby the Turks recognized the protectorate of the Russian tsar over Serbia. The rights guaranteed under the Treaty of Bucharest were more clearly defined, with the stipulation that they should enter into effect within a year and a half. Serbia was to remain a Turkish dependency, but with complete autonomy, and Turks were to be allowed to reside in only eight garrison towns.

Milosh announced these terms at a great *skupshtina* held at Kraguyevatz in January, 1827, but the Turks, according to their usual practice, refused to execute it when it came to a showdown. A few months later Great Britain, France, and Russia demanded an armistice preliminary to settling the Greek question, which had been acute since 1821. When the sultan refused to accept the mediation of these powers, the allied fleet fought and won the battle of Navarino, in which the Turkish fleet was destroyed. Then, since the Turks still refused to carry out the Akerman convention, Nicholas I declared war. His forces crossed the Danube, and by the capture of Varna, the Bulgarian port, opened the road to the Balkans. The peace concluded at Adrianople in 1829 reaffirmed and applied the terms of the Treaty of Bucharest. At last these conditions were carried out. Milosh was later recognized by the sultan as hereditary prince of Serbia, the territory of which included most of

Servitude and Liberation 169

its area before 1914, that is, from the Save and the Danube southward between Drina and Timok as far as Nish, though Bosnia, Herzegovina, Novipazar, and Macedonia remained in Turkish possession.

Milosh accomplished much for Serbia, but became increasingly unpopular because of his autocratic methods and bearing among an essentially democratic people, with the result that in 1835 a constitution was forced on the country by the tsar and the sultan jointly. The prince was irritated by this restriction of his hitherto absolute power, and even engineered a popular protest against it. For this reason, he was forced in 1839 to abdicate in favor of his son Milan, and retired to his extensive estates in Romania. After the untimely death of Milan, the council of state chose as Prince Milosh's second son Mikhailo, then but sixteen years of age. He met with Turkish opposition, however, and was replaced in 1843 by Alexander, the son of old Karageorge, the hero of the early wars of liberation. During his reign, after the Crimean War, the Treaty of Paris (1856) abolished the Russian protectorate and placed Serbia, along with the other Balkan communities, under the joint protection of the Great Powers, while all Turkish armed intervention in Serbian domestic affairs was henceforth forbidden.

Alexander was in constant conflict with the council of state, some members of which even conspired against him, but he was ultimately forced by the Turks to cancel the sentences against the convicted conspirators. Under pressure from his advisors and from a large section of the populace, Alexander in 1859 convoked the first elected *skupshtina* (all previous ones had been appointive), which voted his removal and invited old Milosh Obrenovich to return.

Upon his resumption of the principate, Milosh revived his previous autocratic tactics, disregarded the wishes of the assembly that had recalled him, and was none too scrupulous in his attitude toward the public treasury. In 1860, during negotiations for the evacuation of the Turkish garrison towns,

Milosh died and was succeeded again by his son Mikhailo, who had gained discretion with years, and proved to be one of the best rulers Serbia ever had. His administrative reforms all aimed at increased independence from Turkey and at intensified democracy.

Relations with Turkey soon became strained once more as a result of an insurrection in Herzegovina. Early in the summer of 1861 a street brawl in Belgrade developed into a general *mêlée* between Turkish soldiery and Serbian populace, culminating in the bombardment of the city by the Turkish commander of the fortress. With the support of the Powers, offended by this incident, Mikhailo secured a promise that all but four Turkish garrisons should be evacuated. Egged on by the Austrians, however, the Turks delayed executing these stipulations until the outbreak of the war between Prussia and Austria, when Mikhailo secured British and Russian backing for his demand that all remaining Turkish garrisons should be withdrawn, and that Turkish civilians should also leave Serbia. Handicapped by events in Bosnia, Herzegovina, and Bulgaria, the Turks were in no state to resist, so that the last four fortresses were surrendered on April 6, 1867.

At the national assembly convoked on the following October, Mikhailo could thus truthfully declare, "The Turkish garrisons have been removed from Serbia; the cities on the banks of the Save and the Danube are in our hands, and the freedom and the domestic independence of Serbia have become a firm reality." Mikhailo now proceeded to aid in the liberation of the other oppressed Balkan Slavs, supporting with funds the rebels in Bosnia, Herzegovina, and Bulgaria, beside projecting an alliance with the Greeks. His promising career was cut short by a conspiracy engineered by Austria and Turkey, which resulted in his assassination on May 29, 1868. Since Mikhailo died childless, the principate was passed by a vote of a special national assembly to his sixteen-year-old cousin Milan Obrenovich, who at the time was a student in Paris. There was to be a regency of three members till his majority in 1872. Milan proved neither gifted nor industrious, though during the regency a new constitution was elaborated (1869) which introduced the principle of ministerial responsibility.

At this period, the disorder and violence prevalent in Turkish territory once more stirred Bosnia and Herzegovina to revolt, which aroused such intense popular sympathy in Serbia that in 1876 Milan was obliged against his will to declare war on Turkey. The Serbian military establishment was too ill-equipped to withstand the well-organized Turkish forces, which before long had gained so much ground that the Serbs were obliged to call on Russia for intervention. The Turkish advance down the Morava was thus halted by the peace of 1877 which restored the status quo.

This peace was of short duration, for within a few months Russia was itself at war with Turkey, and during the ensuing campaign the Russian troops advanced as far south as Adrianople, which they captured in January 1878. Simultaneously the Serbs moved southward through Nish to Kossovo, which they had not traversed as victors since the tragic defeat of 1359, and the Montenegrins captured several strongholds on the Adriatic seaboard. Though the Treaty of San Stefano, extracted by the Russians from the Turks at the point of the bayonet, was rejected by the Great Powers, the settlement later arrived at by the Congress of Berlin entailed great gains for Serbia. With Montenegro, it now became for the first time totally independent of the Turks, and was territorially increased by the acquisition of the southern areas which it had conquered during the campaign. Montenegro was given the sections it had won by hard fighting in the interior together with a small coastline which included the insignificant and practically useless ports of Antivari and Dulcigno. It was, however, a major catastrophe that the so-called Sanjak of Novipazar, the cradle of Serbian independence (for it was none other than the medieval principality of Rashka, from which Stephen Nemanya's expansion had begun in the twelfth century) was turned over to Austrian occupation and remained a thorn in the side of the Serbs until 1918. Serbia's arrival at full statehood was then consecrated by Milan's assumption of the royal title in 1882, though seldom did a crown grace the head of a less competent monarch, as his later reign and marital entanglements amply proved.

The subsequent evolution of Serbia belongs to phases of modern political and economic history which lie beyond our scope. But in the seven hundred years of Serbian history which we have treated, we have seen the rise, fall, and rebirth of a singularly gifted and instinctively democratic people, handicapped both by their own individualism and by the depressing effects of foreign domination and intrigue, who in our own day, after being territorially reunited, passed through the throes of a military dictatorship and then returned to the practice of democracy before World War II.

Bulgaria, on account of its geographical situation and accessibility, was more completely reduced to subjection than Serbia, and thus was slower to emancipate itself. In this process the Bulgarians, like the Serbs, were aided by the Russian offensive against the Turks, which began under Catherine II in 1771, and was successfully continued by Kutuzov's operations on the lower Danube in 1811, which culminated in the Peace of Bucharest. After a long interruption during the Napoleonic wars and the latter part of Alexander I's reign, operations against the Turks were resumed in 1827 by his brother and successor Nicholas I. The subsequent Convention of Akerman and Treaty of Adrianople are already familiar from the course of Serbian history, but were of no practical benefit to Bulgaria. As early as 1852, however, Nicholas had plans for the independence of Serbia and Bulgaria, but met with the concerted opposition of England and France, which feared any expansion of Russian influence at Stambul and were ready even to drive Russia out of the Danube provinces of Walachia and Moldavia, which the Russians had occupied during the summer of 1853. This occupation led up to the Crimean War, which broke out the next year. A joint Anglo-French expeditionary

Servitude and Liberation 173

force reached Varna in Bulgaria, whereupon the Russians abandoned the Danube provinces, which were then occupied by the Austrians. As we have seen, the international settlement after the Crimean War resulted in the Russian renunciation of the previous protectorate over the Orthodox subjects of the sultan.

During the first twenty years of the reign of Alexander II, Russia was too engrossed in the great reforms and in Asiatic expansion to play an influential role in Turkish affairs. But in 1875 the Bosnian uprising and its accompanying events attracted general European attention, especially after the terrible massacres which followed a Bulgarian revolt in sympathy with the Bosnian rebellion. Russia secured Austrian support for Russian intervention at the price of a promise that Bosnia and Herzegovina should fall to Austria if action were taken. The tsar also informed the British that he would occupy no more than Bulgaria. Still apprehensive of a possible growth of Russian prestige in the Balkans, the London government made every effort to put through a peaceful solution, but was handicapped by the obstinacy of the Turks, so that the Russians, whose public opinion was now wildly excited over the fate of their Orthodox kin, declared war against Turkey in April, 1877.

Since the Russian army was not particularly efficient, progress was slow, but during the next winter the Russians captured Sofia and, after crossing the Balkan chain, took Adrianople in January, 1878, and reached the seacoast. Within two weeks British intervention produced an armistice, since the English were resolved not to tolerate a Russian occupation of Stambul. The Treaty of San Stefano, concluded between Russia and Turkey in March, 1878, created a Bulgarian principality which would have extended from the Danube to the Aegean, including the whole of Macedonia as far as Albania. This principality was to be ruled by a Christian prince who, though a Turkish vassal, would have been supported by a Russian commissioner backed by a Russian occupationary force of fifty thousand men. Here again British jealousy of Russia came into play, with the result that by the Berlin Conference all these arrangements were scrapped. Bulgaria between the Balkan mountains and the Danube became an autonomous state under Turkish sovereignty. It was deprived of any Aegean coastline, since the area south of the Balkans, now termed Eastern Rumelia, was to remain subject to Turkish rule under a Christian governor to be appointed by the sultan. Macedonia stayed in Turkish hands, and the Dobrudja, the area between the Black Sea and the lower Danube, was allotted to Romania. Southern Bessarabia, held by Romania since the Treaty of Paris (1856) was returned to Russia.

Despite its complex racial background, Bulgaria was socially an extremely homogenous nation. Primarily agricultural, it consisted almost entirely of peasants, with no middle class and no intelligentsia, while the church, as we have seen, had been exclusively under Greek control since the abolition of the independent patriarchates in 1767. Such intellectual development as took place during the first fifty years of the last century was sponsored by wealthy Bulgarian merchants resident in Bucharest and Odessa. The committees formed in the Bulgarian interest at these centers represented opposite poles: the Romanian committee favored peaceful regeneration, while the Russian advocated direct action with violence if necesary. The first Bulgarian school was established in 1835. The first actual step at intellectual emancipation was the divorce of the Bulgarian Church from the patriarchate of Constantinople in 1860, followed by the establishment of the Bulgarian exarchate twelve years later, though the exarch himself resided in Stambul till 1908.

The Bulgarians, though indebted to the Russians for the freedom they enjoyed, resented Russian pretentions to dominating influence. The Bulgarians also, perhaps on account of their mixed blood, always felt themselves a shade above their Slavic neighbors in the Balkans. Dynastic affiliations (two successive German princes) doubtless played some role in the gradual alienation of Bulgaria from general Slavic aims and ideals, and contributed to the closer contact which long prevailed between Bulgaria and the German powers of the Triple Alliance before 1914. Economically also, in view of railroad connections and the avenue of trade into Central Europe provided by the Danube, the practical interests of Bulgaria drew it away from Russia. This fact also applies to Serbia, and would have been a stronger influence had the Austrians before 1914 ever been disposed to give the Serbs an economic square deal. And further, the Bulgarians had traditional designs on Constantinople which made them potential opponents of the Russian hope for possession of the Straits themselves.

After the conclusion of the Treaty of Berlin, the first Bulgarian constitutional assembly convened at Tirnovo on February 10, 1879. Though efforts were made to impose a conservative document which would have given the landholders, capitalists, and small middle class a dominant influence, the result was an extremely democratic fundamental law based generally on the accepted British principles of constitutional monarchy. While the constitutional assembly was still sitting, a national assembly was elected by popular vote, which chose as Prince Alexander of Battenberg, who assumed office on June 25. Alexander resisted the paramount Russian influence to the best of his ability but, after trying and abandoning a dictatorial policy, he was constantly in hot water with the domestic political parties. In 1885, he successfully carried through the annexation of Eastern Rumelia, and resisted with good results the Serbian attack which followed, but was forced to abdicate the following summer by Russophile elements in the army. Though returned to power barely a week later by a counterrevolutionary movement headed by the liberal leader Stephen Stambulov, Alexander had lost the support of the Russians, who again forced him to retire.

Stambulov, who was an intense Russophobe, now became practically dictator, and engineered the election of Ferdinand of Saxe-Coburg as Prince of Bulgaria. Leaving the reins of government in the hands of the domineering Stambulov, Ferdinand concentrated his efforts on strengthening his diplomatic standing. When Stambulov was assassinated and Tsar Alexander III died in 1894, a reconciliation with Russia followed, with the sultan recognizing Ferdinand as prince of Bulgaria and governor-general of eastern Rumelia. Ferdinand's reign was also marked by a rapid economic advance. At the beginning of the present century, conditions in Turkey became so chaotic as to produce the Young Turk revolution of 1908, in the course of which Ferdinand proclaimed the independence of Bulgaria and assumed the title of tsar. A third independent Slavic state was thus established in the Balkans, though Bosnia and Herzegovina were formally annexed by Austria-Hungary, which also retained under its sway a large population of Slovenes, Croats, Czechs, Slovaks, Poles, and Ruthenians, whose liberation was to follow ten years later at the close of the first World War.

gressive industrialization of the world and the need of reapportioning both essential raw materials and export markets, there are already enough problems confronting the major nations in their dealings with one another without the risk of becoming embroiled over the petty aspirations, mistakes, and quarrels of these minor units.

During the last century and a half there has been much discussion of the so-called missions of the various nations. This altruistic concept of the romantic philosophers derives from the conviction that each nation has a role to play in the progress of the world and is destined to bring something new to its fellows. It originated in the observation that different nations arrive at various degrees of political, material, or intellectual advancement at different times, and their innovations and accomplishments are then passed along to their contemporaries. Herder thus wrote in 1774, "The Slavs are destined to say the last word in the development of European humanity." The great Italian patriot Mazzini added in 1861, "The Slavic movement comes next to the Italian movement in importance for the future of Europe. If this movement is helped and hailed as a providential occurrence, it will rejuvenate the life of Europe by new impulses and potentialities." Even Nietzsche declared, "Modern Germany is an advance post of the Slavic world and prepared the way for a pan-Slavic Europe."

I submit that this is romantic nonsense. The same notion of a national mission lay behind the dynamics of the Nazi party and is equally fallacious. Insofar as any nation at the present day can be said to have a mission, it consists in assuring the maximum prosperity for its members, in refraining from acts which antagonize its neighbors, and in contributing by its native gifts to the sum total of human progress. No nation has a mission of aggression at the expense of others, and the Slavs least of all. But they do have a right to evolve and develop their native talents under a maximum of liberty. The fruits of their talents will then be transmitted in due course to the world at large, just as Russian literature and music have become the prized possession of an international public. Unfortunately, however, the Slavs in Central Europe are so placed geographically that individual states based on purely linguistic frontiers are not economically self-sufficient, while frontiers which do not follow linguistic boundaries perpetuate the struggle between German and Slav.

INDEX

Adalbert, bishop of Prague, 67
Adrian II, Pope, 59, 61
Adrianople, 152, 155, 159, 160, 168, 171, 172, 173
Adriatic Sea, 28, 30, 31, 54, 61, 144, 145, 146, 147, 152, 157, 167, 171
Aegean Sea, 28, 33, 146, 173
Akerman, Convention of, 168, 172
Albania, 145, 148, 152, 159, 173
Albert von Ballenstedt, Margrave of the Nordmark, 130
Alevisio Novi, 104
Alexander of Battenberg, Prince, 175
Alexander the Great, 12, 13
Alexander, son of Karageorge, 169
Alexander I of Russia, 113, 166, 172
Alexander II of Russia, 114, 116, 117
Alexander III of Russia, 175
Alexander Nevsky, Prince, 134
Alexis, Tsar, 108, 109
America, 99, 151
Andrew, King of Hungary, 79
Andrew, Prince, 84, 94
Andronicus III, 148
Angelus, Alexius, Emperor, 146, 158
Angelus, Isaac, 157, 158
Angelus, Manuel, 158, 159
Angelus, Michael, 146
Angelus, Theodore, 146, 147, 159
Anna, daughter of Theodore Angelus, 147
Anna, Empress of Russia, 110, 111
Anna, Princess, 68, 69, 70, 156
Antivari, 147, 151, 171
Aquileia, 54
Arkona, 25
Asen dynasty, 180
Asen, John, 157
Asen, John, II, 158, 159, 160

Asen, Peter, 157, 158
Asia, 21, 75, 85
Asia Minor, 12, 145, 157
Astrakhan, 91
Atlantic Ocean, 10, 130
Attica, 30
Attila, 28, 31
Augsburg, 122
Austria, 122, 123, 127, 139, 143, 165, 167, 170, 181
Austria, Duchy of, 122
Austria-Hungary, 139, 140, 176, 181
Avignon, 149
Azov, Sea of, 85

Bakunin, Mikhail, 114
Balaton, Lake, 54, 55, 59
Baldwin, son of Robert de Courtenay, 159
Baldwin I, Latin Emperor of Byzantium, 158
Baldwin II, 159
Balkan peninsula, 30, 32, 33, 143, 154, 177
Balkans, 23, 26, 29, 30, 31, 33, 40, 41, 45, 47, 57, 61, 144, 155, 158, 174, 176, 182
Baltic coast, 3, 5, 14, 46, 49, 65, 84, 121, 133, 178, 179, 180
Baltic Sea, 7, 11, 14, 28, 36, 67, 73, 76, 79, 178, 179
Bamberg, 123
Banat, 161
Barbarossa, Frederick, 158
Basil I, Emperor of Byzantium, 61, 62, 63, 88, 89
Basil II, Emperor of Byzantium, 68, 69, 71, 89, 90, 91, 95, 96, 104, 157
Basil III, Grand Prince of Moscow, 91, 96
Batory, Stephen, 135

Batu, grandson of Genghis Khan, 85
Bautzen, 131
Bavaria, 32, 123
Bayazid, 152, 160
Belgrade, 61, 63, 144, 145, 153, 155, 161, 164, 166, 167, 170
Belinski, Vissarion, 114
Beneš, Eduard, 182
Berezina River, 39, 49
Berlin, 128, 129, 171, 174, 175
Berrhoea, 157
Beskids, 37
Bessarabia, 174
Bialystok, 2
Black Sea, 2, 7, 8, 11, 12, 14, 15, 19, 20, 23, 28, 31, 39, 40, 42, 47, 48, 67, 77, 88, 89, 92, 134, 157
Blasius, Saint, 25
Bobbio, 53
Bober River, 38, 66, 130, 131
Bocche di Cattaro, 167
Bohemia, 32, 37, 55, 121, 124, 125, 127, 128, 136, 137, 139, 140, 141, 144, 178, 181
Böhmer Wald, 37
Boileau, 111
Bokhara, 91
Boleslav I, Prince, 66, 130
Boleslav the Brave of Poland, 66, 67, 131
Boris, Prince of Bulgaria, 56, 57, 60, 62, 63, 70, 72, 74, 154, 180
Boris Godunov, 105, 107
Bosnia, 143, 144, 145, 151, 152, 153, 154, 161, 162, 164, 166, 169, 170, 171, 176, 182
Bosporus, 63, 149
Boyana River, 145
Brandenburg, 126, 129, 130, 132, 135, 136
Branibor, 128
Brankovich, George, 153
Bratislava, 37, 122
Bregenz, 53
Brennus, 5
Breslau, 67, 132, 133
Brest-Litovsk, 2, 39, 49

Bucharest, Peace of, 167, 168, 172, 174
Bug River, 7, 8, 13, 14, 15, 38, 41, 48
Bukovina, 2, 47
Bulgaria, 33, 40, 58, 61, 63, 64, 67, 68, 70, 71, 79, 147, 148, 151, 154, 155, 156, 157, 160, 172, 173, 174, 175, 176, 178, 180, 182
Byelorussia (White Russia), 46, 88
Byzantium, 23, 29, 42, 47, 57, 60, 61, 62, 64, 65, 67, 68, 70, 72, 74, 76, 78, 81, 83, 84, 96, 98, 99, 102, 103, 144, 147, 148, 149, 154, 155, 156, 157, 179

Calvin, 99
Caracalla, 15
Carinthia, 32, 53, 54, 122, 123, 167
Carloman, Margrave of Ostmark, 56, 57
Carniola, 32, 53, 54, 123, 143
Carpathian Mountains, 5, 6, 7, 8, 11, 29, 32, 37, 39, 42, 48, 177
Caspian Sea, 16, 84
Catherine II of Russia, 91, 111, 112, 165, 172
Caucasus, 19, 40, 49
Central Europe, 20, 24, 41, 145, 155, 175, 178, 182, 185
Central Russia, 46, 177
Charlemagne, 31, 35, 36, 54, 55, 101, 122, 124, 128, 129
Charles IV of Bohemia, 149
Charles X, King of Sweden, 136
Châteaubriand, 138
Chekhov, Anton, 116
Chernigov, 49, 77, 84, 85
Chersonesus, 69
Chmelnitski, Bogdan, 136
Clement, disciple of Methodius, 63, 64, 154
Columban, Saint, 53
Columbus, 99
Comnenus, Manuel, Emperor of Byzantium, 145
Conrad I of Germany, 128
Conrad II of Germany, 131
Conrad, Duke of Mazovia, 132

Constantine, 57, 58, 59, 60, 63, 64, 65, 68, 69, 71, 73, 123, 124, 154, 178, 180
Constantine, Prince, 159, 160
Constantine Porphyrogenitus, Emperor of Byzantium, 68, 79
Constantinople, 28, 29, 30, 57, 61, 62, 63, 67, 68, 69, 71, 77, 78, 79, 90, 96, 99, 101, 144, 146, 148, 149, 153, 154, 155, 156, 158, 159, 174, 175, 178, 179. *See also* Stambul
Constantinople, Straits of, 175
Coolidge, Archibald Cary, 183
Corneille, Pierre, 110
Courland, 135
Courtenay, Robert de, Latin Emperor of Byzantium, 159
Cracow, 37, 67, 132, 133, 141, 147
Crete, 30
Crimea, 7, 11, 15, 16, 78, 84, 90
Croatia, 64, 65, 145, 151, 154, 161, 167
Cyril, Saint, *see* Constantine
Czechoslovakia, 2, 36, 55, 139, 182
Czernowitz, 3

Dacia, 14
Dalmatia, 29, 30, 61, 143, 145, 149, 151, 154, 161, 162, 164
Dandolo of Venice, Doge Enrico, 146
Danube Basin, 8, 26, 29, 33, 40, 122, 177
Danube River, 4, 5, 12, 19, 23, 27, 29, 30, 32, 33, 34, 37, 38, 41, 48, 53, 54, 55, 56, 61, 63, 65, 121, 122, 123, 128, 144, 152, 153, 154, 156, 158, 164, 165, 166, 167, 169, 170, 172, 173, 174, 178, 180
Danzig, 3, 36, 38, 46, 132, 135, 136
Danzig, corridor of, 183
Delphi, 5
Denmark, 35
Deodoricus, 54
Desna River, 4, 39, 49
Diagilev, 119
Dmitri Donskoi, Prince, 87, 88, 104
Dneprostroi Dam, 156

Dnieper River, 4, 7, 11, 12, 13, 14, 15, 21, 23, 39, 41, 42, 48, 49, 50, 69, 76, 77, 78, 79, 81, 85, 92, 108, 177, 178, 179
Dniester River, 7, 8, 13, 15, 27, 38, 41, 42, 47, 48
Dobrudja, 174
Don Juan of Austria, 154, 164
Don River, 2, 12, 13, 28, 39, 40, 41, 45, 47, 49, 85, 88
Donetz River, 39
Dostoevski, Feodor, 114, 115, 118
Drave River, 29, 32, 54, 62, 123, 144, 145, 161
Dresden, 3, 36
Drin River, 154
Drina River, 144, 152, 169
Dubravka, 66, 130
Dubrovski, Joseph, 138
Dulcigno, 171
Durazzo, 32
Dushan, Stephen, 147, 148, 149, 150, 151, 154, 160, 180
Dvina River, 4, 7, 14, 39, 49, 50, 133

East Prussia, 7, 39, 46, 66, 134, 136
Eger, district of, 124
Elbe River, 7, 23, 28, 34, 35, 36, 65, 66, 73, 121, 127, 128, 129, 130, 131, 132, 136, 177, 180
Elbing, 132
Elizabeth, Empress of Russia, 110, 111, 136
Elizabeth, Queen of England, 79
England, 99, 172
Enns, 53
Epirus, 30, 34, 146, 148, 151, 158
Ermanaric, 23
Erzgebirge, 37
Esthonia, 85, 92, 134, 135
Eudoxia, Princess, 146
Eugene IV, Pope, 104
Eugene, Prince of Savoy, 164

Fallmerayer, 34
Ferdinand of Saxe-Coburg, 175, 176
Finland, Gulf of, 14, 46, 92, 133, 180

Fioravanti, Rudolfo, 104
Fiume, 144
Flanders, 126
Florence, 104, 147
Fonvisin, Denis, 112
France, 99, 168, 172
Franconia, 123
Frankfurt on the Oder, 38, 130
Frankfurt-Glogau, 66
Freising, 60, 123

Galicia, 2, 39, 47, 79, 85, 86, 133, 136, 141, 142, 179
Galicia-Volhynia, principality of, 86
Gallipoli, 149
Genghis Khan, 84, 85
George, son of Vladimir Monomakh, 83
George II, Prince of Suzdal, 85
Germany, 26, 35, 65, 124, 136, 182
Gero, German Margrave, 66
Gesenke, 37
Gnesen, see Gniezno
Gnezdovo, 75
Gniezno, 38, 67, 131, 133
Goethe, Wolfgang von, 137
Gogol, Nicholas, 114
Gorazd, 62
Gorki, Maxim, 117
Great Britain, 168
Great Russia, 86
Greece, 5, 72, 168
Greek Peninsula, 30, 33, 61
Grek, Maxim, 105
Grodno, 2
Grünwald-Tannenberg, Battle of, 89, 134
Gulf of Riga, 7, 39, 46, 92
Gytha, 80

Halle, 128
Hamburg, 35, 36, 126, 128
Hapsburgs, 73, 181
Harald the Severe, King of Norway, 79
Harold the Saxon, 80
Hartz Mountains, 128
Hastings, 80

Havel, 128
Hegel, 114, 181
Hellas, 34
Hellespont, 160
Henry the Fowler, 128, 129
Henry I, King of France, 79
Henry II of Germany, 131
Henry, Duke of Saxony, see Henry the Fowler
Herder, Johann Gottfried, 137, 138, 184
Hermanarich, Bishop of Passau, 60
Hermann, Vladislav, 132
Herodotus, 6, 12, 14
Herzegovina, 144, 153, 154, 161, 166, 169, 170, 171, 176, 182
Herzen, Alexander, 114
High Tatra, 37
Hindustan, 10
Hitler, Adolf, 182
Holstein, 129
Holy Roman Empire, 140
Hungary, 26, 29, 36, 49, 139, 145, 147, 149, 151, 152, 153, 154, 161, 164, 182
Hunyadi, John, 153
Hus, Jan, 99

Ibar River, 145, 154
Illyria, 30
Ilmen, Lake, 4, 39, 47, 50
Ingigerd, 79
Innocent III, Pope, 158
Innocent VI, Pope, 149
Ipek, see Peć
Istria, 30, 32
Italy, 53, 99, 152
Itil, 42
Ivan I, Prince of Moscow, 87
Ivan III, Grand Prince of Moscow, 90, 91, 95, 96, 104, 106, 109, 134
Ivan IV, the Terrible, Tsar of Moscow, 91, 92, 97, 104, 105, 108, 134, 179
Ivor, 76
Iziaslav, Prince of Kiev, 81

Jablunka, 37

Index

Jagailo, Prince, 89, 134
Jagiellonczyk, Kazimir, 135
Jena, 138
John VIII, Pope, 61, 62
Jordanes, 5, 15, 27, 28, 29
Joseph II, Emperor of Austria, 137, 165
Julius Capitolinus, 35
Jungmann, Joseph, 138
Justinian, Emperor of Byzantium, 26
Jutland, peninsula of, 121

Kalka River, 84, 85
Kaloyan of Bulgaria, 158
Kama River, 41
Karageorge (Black George Petrovich), 165, 166, 167
Karelia, 85
Karlish, 133
Karlovcy, Treaty of, 164
Kazan, 14, 85, 90, 91
Kazimir the Great, King of Poland, 89, 134
Kazimov, 90
Kerch, 42
Khazaria, 57, 58
Khilander Monastery, 146
Khiva, 91
Kiel, 36, 129
Kiev, 3, 4, 7, 12, 25, 39, 42, 47, 48, 49, 50, 64, 67, 68, 69, 70, 72, 73, 75, 76, 77, 78, 79, 80, 81, 82, 83, 84, 85, 86, 88, 92, 93, 94, 96, 99, 100, 102, 108, 109, 134, 156, 158, 179
Klyazma River, 86
Kola peninsula, 93
Kolberg (Pomerania), 67
Kollár, Joseph, 138
Königsberg, 7, 46, 132
Kossovo Polje (Magpie's Field), 152, 160, 171
Kotzel, Prince, 56, 59, 60
Kraguyevatz, 168
Krain, *see* Carniola
Krakow, *see* Cracow
Kremlin, 51, 90, 104

Kuban, district of, 19, 40
Kuban River, 2
Kubrat, Prince, 40
Kuibyshev (Samara), 117
Kulikovo Polye (Snipe Field), 88
Kulm, 132
Kursk, 49
Kustendil, 144
Kutuzov, Prince, 167, 172

Laba, *see* Elbe
Ladoga, Lake, 39, 50, 75, 178
Laibach (Ljubljana), 143
Larissa, 157
Lascaris, Theodore, 146
Latvia, 46
Lausitz, *see* Lusatia,
Lazarevich, Stephen, 153
Lechfeld, 122
Leipzig, 111
Lemberg (Lvóv), 133, 136, 141
Lenin, Nicholas, 117
Leopold II, Emperor of Austria, 165
Lepanto, Battle of, 154, 164
Lermontov, Mikhail, 113
Levant, 133
Liegnitz, 85
Linz, 37
Lithuania, 46, 88, 90, 92, 96, 108, 134, 179
Livonia, 133, 134, 135
Lomonosov, Mikhail, 111
Lothar, Duke of Saxony, 129
Louis of Hungary, King, 89, 149
Louis the German, King, 55, 56, 57, 59, 60, 61
Louis the Pious, King, 54, 55, 128
Lovat River, 14, 39, 50
Lubech, 77, 129, 133
Lublin, 133
Lusatia, 3, 36, 130, 131
Luther, Martin, 99
Lutsk, 47
Lyudevit, Prince, 54

Macedonia, 5, 30, 31, 33, 34, 61, 63, 144, 148, 149, 152, 155, 156, 159, 161, 169, 173, 174

Index

Magdeburg, 35, 66, 131
Mainz, 67
Mamai, Tartar Khan, 88
Marcus Aurelius, 35, 122
Maria, sister of Yaroslav of Kiev, 79
Maria Theresa, Empress of Austria, 165
Maritza River, 152
Marx, Karl, 114
Masaryk, Thomas, 182
Matveyev, Artamon, 108
Maximilian, Emperor, 91
Mazovia, 132
Mazzini, Giuseppe, 184
Mediterranean Sea, 10, 21, 78
Meissen, 128, 131, 132
Memel, 7, 89
Methodius, 57, 59, 60, 61, 62, 63, 64, 65, 71, 73, 123, 124, 125, 154, 178, 180
Metternich, Prince, 139
Michael III of Byzantium (the Drunkard), 56, 58, 61
Michael, Prince of Tver, 87
Michael, tsar of Russia, 107
Mieszko I, Prince of Poland, 66, 74, 130, 131
Mikhailo, son of Milosh Obrenovich, 169, 170
Milan, son of Milosh Obrenovich, 169
Minsk, 2, 51
Moesia, 33, 41
Mohammed II, 153
Mojmir, 55
Moldavia, 45, 162, 172
Molière, 110
Mongolia, 16, 40
Montenegro, 147, 161, 164, 166, 171
Morava River, 4, 37, 61, 144, 145, 152, 153, 154, 155, 165, 171
Moravia, 28, 32, 37, 56, 58, 60, 62, 64, 73, 121, 123, 124, 131, 154, 178
Mosaburg, 55
Moscow, 46, 49, 50, 75, 85, 86, 87, 88, 89, 90, 91, 92, 94, 95, 98, 102, 104, 108, 109, 167, 179
Moscow River, 46

Moselle River, 122
Mount Athos, 57, 105, 145
Mount Olympus, 58
Mstislav, Prince, 84, 85
Mur River, 123, 143
Murad, Sultan of Turkey, 152, 160
Murom, 77, 83
Myriokephalon, 145

Napoleon, 167
Narenta River, 145, 152
Narev River, 8
Narishkina, Natalia, 108
Narva, 92
Navarino, Battle of, 168
Neisse River, 37
Nemanya, Stephen, 145, 158, 159, 171, 180
Nemanyich, Anna, 146
Nemanyich, Stephen, 146, 158
Nemanyich, Vukan, 146, 158
Netze River, 38, 135
Neva River, 39
Nicaea, 146, 159
Nicephorus Phocas, 155, 156
Nicholas I, Emperor of Russia, 113, 168, 172
Nicholas II, Emperor of Russia, 116
Nicholas I, Pope, 59
Niemen River, 49
Nietzsche, Friedrich, 184
Nish, 144, 152, 153, 155, 158, 166, 169, 171
Nordgau, 124
Norway, 79
Notecz River, *see* Netze
Novgorod, 4, 50, 51, 67, 76, 77, 79, 83, 85, 90, 91, 93, 95, 102, 134
Novikov, Nicholas, 112
Novipazar, 145, 151, 166, 169
Nystadt, Peace of, 135

Ob River, 45
Obrenovich, Milan, 170, 171, 172
Obrenovich, Milosh, 167, 168, 169, 170
Oda, daughter of Margrave Thiedrich, 66

Index

Oder River, 34, 35, 36, 37, 38, 65, 66, 129, 130, 136
Odessa, 7, 174
Odo, Margrave, 66
Oka River, 14, 39, 47, 49, 75, 83, 90, 91
Okhrida, 64, 154, 160, 161, 162
Olaf Haraldsson, King of Norway, 79
Oleg, Prince of Kiev, 76
Olga, Princess of Kiev, 67, 78
Olgerd, Prince of Lithuania, 88, 89
Omurtag, 56
Onega, Lake, 50
Orient, 24, 76, 179
Ostmark, 56, 122
Otto I, King of Germany, 65, 66, 68, 122, 124, 129, 130, 131, 156
Otto III, King of Germany, 66, 67, 131

Palacký, Francis, 138, 139
Palaeologa, Zoe (Sophia), 90
Palaeologi, 147
Palaeologus, Emperor John V, 148
Palaeologus, Emperor Michael, 160
Pannonia, 28, 45, 54, 60, 61, 64
Paris, Treaty of, 169, 174
Passau, 55, 56, 59, 60, 123
Peć (Ipek), 150, 162
Peipus, Lake, 134
Peloponnese, 30
Pereslavl, 49
Peter the Great, 92, 98, 100, 103, 104, 108, 109, 110, 111, 112, 180
Peter Mogila, 109
Phanagoria, 42
Philip of Macedon, 177
Philippopolis (Plovdiv), 155
Photius, Patriarch of Constantinople, 57, 62, 63
Pindus, 31
Pinsk, 49
Pirot, 144
Pittsburgh, Treaty of, 182
Pléiade, 99
Pliny the Elder, 5, 8
Pliska, 63

Podolia, 14
Poland, 19, 36, 66, 86, 89, 91, 92, 108, 109, 113, 131, 132, 133, 134, 135, 136, 137, 140, 144, 150, 153, 178, 181, 183
Polot River, 4
Polotzk, 50
Polychron Monastery, 58
Pomerania, 66, 135
Pomerelia, 132
Pomorze, 132, 135
Pozen, see Poznan
Poznan, 38, 66, 67, 130, 133, 135, 136, 141
Prague, 124, 125, 137, 139
Prague, University of, 137
Preslav, 155, 156
Pressburg, see Bratislava
Pribina, Margrave, 54, 55, 56
Pripet River, 4, 8, 15, 39, 48, 49
Priscus, 28
Prizren, 145, 151
Procopius, 26, 35
Prussia, 136, 167, 170
Prut River, 8, 32, 47
Przemysl, 2, 133
Pskov, 50, 91, 93, 134
Ptolemy, Claudius, 5
Pushkin, Alexander, 111, 113

Quedlinburg, 66, 131

Racine, Jean, 110
Radishchev, Alexander, 111
Radoslav, son of Stephen Nemanyich, 146, 147
Ragusa (Dubrovnik), 31, 145, 148, 151, 154, 162
Rashka, 145, 158, 171
Regensburg, 35, 55, 59, 123, 124
Rhine River, 19, 34, 122, 128
Rhineland, 123, 181
Riesengebirge, 33
Riga, 84, 133
Romania, 2, 148, 154, 169, 174
Romanov, family of, 107
Rome, 53, 57, 59, 60, 62, 65, 73, 83, 96, 101, 126, 146, 178
Ronsard, Pierre, 99

Index

Rostislav, Prince of Bohemia, 55, 56, 57, 58, 59, 60
Rostock, 129
Rostov, 77, 83
Rugen, 25
Rumelia, Eastern, 174, 175, 176
Rurik, 76, 77, 107
Russia, South, 11, 12, 33, 42, 45, 70, 90
Russia, Sub-Carpathian, 2, 37, 42, 48
Rustchuck, 167
Ryazan, 47, 85, 90, 91

Saale River, 28, 35, 128, 129
Šafařík, Paul Joseph, 138
St. Petersburg, 110, 116, 117, 118
Saint-Simon, 114
Salona, 32
Salonika, 33, 41, 57, 62, 146, 149, 155, 157, 158, 159
Salzburg, 54, 56, 60, 122
Samo, King of Slovenes, 53
Samuel, Prince of Macedonia, 156, 157, 180
San River, 39
San Stefano, Treaty of, 171, 173
Sanjak of Novipazar, 171
Sarai, 86
Sarajevo, 144, 145, 152
Sardica, *see* Sofia
Save River, 27, 29, 62, 123, 144, 145, 152, 161, 164, 167, 169, 170
Save Valley, 123
Savonarola, 105
Savva, Saint, 145, 146, 150
Saxony, 66, 128
Scandinavia, 10, 35, 45, 47, 75, 80, 100
Scutari, 68, 164
Scutari, Lake, 144
Scythia, 6
Seim River, 39
Sem River, 4
Semendria, 153, 161, 162
Septimius Severus, 23
Serbia, 61, 64, 144, 149, 150, 151, 152, 153, 154, 155, 158, 159, 161, 166, 167, 168, 169, 171, 172, 175, 180, 182

Seret River, 32
Sevastopol, 69
Shishman, John, tsar of Bulgaria, 160
Shumadiya, 165
Siberia, 45, 91, 113
Sidney, Sir Philip, 99
Silesia, 33, 66, 130, 131, 132, 136
Silistria, 156
Simeon the Great, of Bulgaria, 63, 64, 70, 72, 74, 154, 155, 157, 180
Simeon Polotski, 109
Sineus, 76
Sirmium, 144
Skoplje, 147, 149, 152, 158
Slavonia, 145, 154, 161, 164
Smolensk, 50, 75, 77, 84, 89
Sofia, 155, 173
Sophia, sister of Peter the Great, 109
Soviet Union, 181
Sozh River, 42
Spalato (Split), 144, 147
Spenser, Edmund, 99
Spree River, 3, 36
Spree Valley, 66
Stalin, Joseph, 101
Stalingrad, 86
Stambul (Constantinople), 161, 168, 172, 173. *See also* Constantinople
Stambulov, Stephen, 175, 176
Stephen V, Pope, 62
Stettin, 38
Styria, 32, 54, 123, 143
Sudeten, 27, 32, 37, 66
Sula River, 4
Suzdal, 77, 83, 85, 94, 96
Svatopluk, Prince of Bohemia-Moravia, 60, 62
Sviatoslav, Prince of Kiev, 67, 68, 78, 79, 156
Svidrigailo, Prince of Lithuania, 89
Svishtovo, Treaty of, 165
Sweden, 67, 75, 77, 92, 136
Switzerland, 53
Sylvester II, Pope (Gerbert d'Aurillac), 66
Syria, 157

Tacitus, 5, 8

Index

Tamerlane, 153
Tassilo, Duke of Bavaria, 54
Tatishchev, Basil, 111
Temuchin, see Genghis Khan
Theiss River, 54, 164
Theodore, Tsar of Moscow, 107
Theodosius II, Emperor of Byzantium, 28
Thessaly, 30, 34, 148, 151, 152, 156, 157
Thiedrich, Margrave, 66
Thorn, 132
Thrace, 5, 61, 151, 157, 159, 160
Thuringia, 128, 131
Timok River, 144, 169
Tirnovo, 157, 159, 160, 175
Tokhtamysh, Khan, 89
Tolstoi, Count Leo, 115, 118
Topola, 165
Trajan, 23
Transylvania, 34, 48
Trent, Council of, 135
Trieste, 123, 143
Truvor, 76
Turgenev, Ivan, 114
Turkey, 173, 176
Turov, 49
Tutsa River, 155
Tver, 87, 88, 90
Tyrol, 122
Tzimisces, John, 68, 79, 156

Ugedei, Khan, 85
Ukraine, 12, 49, 51, 75, 88, 108, 109, 113
United States of America, 143
Urosh, Stephen, 147
Václav (Wenceslas), King of Bohemia, 125
Vardar River, 155
Varna, 155, 168, 173
Vatatses, John, of Nicaea, 159
Veglia, 31
Velehrad, 125
Venice, 5, 59, 126, 145, 147, 148, 154, 162
Versailles, Treaty of, 134
Vienna, 37, 85, 123, 139, 164

Vienna, Congress of, 167
Villach, 123
Vistula River, 4, 5, 7, 14, 15, 21, 27, 32, 34, 35, 36, 37, 38, 39, 46, 66, 121, 132, 135, 136, 177, 180
Vitovt, Prince of Lithuania, 89
Vladimir (city), 85, 86, 87, 88, 93, 96, 102, 103
Vladimir I, Saint, Prince of Kiev, 67, 68, 70, 71, 72, 73, 75, 78, 79, 80, 98, 102, 131, 178, 179
Vladimir Monomakh, 82, 83, 94
Vladislav of Serbia, 147, 158, 159
Volga River, 12, 14, 39, 40, 41, 42, 46, 49, 50, 75, 76, 78, 79, 83, 85, 86, 91, 179
Volhynia, 2, 14, 15, 39, 47, 66, 79, 84, 86, 88
Volkhov River, 39, 50
Vsevolod, son of Prince Yaroslav of Kiev, 79
Vsevolod the Big Nest, Prince of Kiev, 84

Walachia, 29, 34, 162, 172
Warsaw, 38, 132, 133
Warta River, 38, 135
Warthe River, see Warta River
Wehlau, Treaty of, 136
Weser River, 128, 136
Western Europe, 77, 91, 98, 99, 100, 137, 142, 152
Westphalia, Peace of, 136
White Russia, see Byelorussia
White Sea, 92, 93, 111
Wiching, 62
Wilzi, 128
Wittenberg, 129
Würzburg, 128
Wyclif, John, 99

Yadwiga, Queen of Poland, 89, 134
Yaroslav the Wise, Prince of Kiev, 71, 79, 80, 81, 83
Yugoslavia, 3, 143

Zara, 144
Zeta (Montenegro), 145, 154

IX

Conclusion

We have thus traced the evolution of the Slavs from their origins to the beginning of the second World War. At the beginning of the Christian era, we found them residing as a loose ethnic unit north of the Carpathian Mountains between the upper course of the Vistula River and the middle reaches of the Russian river Dnieper. We saw them exposed to cultural influences transmitted by Iranian and, still more, by migrant Germanic tribes, but noted that their primitive civilization does not stamp them as an inferior race. There are indications of their early expansion southeast into the steppe country, where they were frequently barred by Asiatic invaders, and to the northeast, where they met little opposition from the Finns of central Russia. Their drift across the Carpathians into the Danube basin was then intensified during the third Christian century, and by the end of the sixth century they had penetrated even further south in the Balkan peninsula than their present area of expansion now extends. After the great German migratory movements between the years 100 and 400 A.D., the Slavs moved west of the Vistula into the area which the removal of the Germanic tribes had left but sparsely settled, until the Western Slavic frontier lay at the Elbe. We noted that even in the proto-Slavic habitat the germs of dialectal differentiation were present, and found that these differences became intensified during the period of Slavic expansion to produce the various Eastern, Western, and Southern Slavic tongues. The subsequent political and cultural history of the Slavs was then conditioned by their locations and by the source from which they assimilated Christianity. The Slavs adjacent to the Danube were, we saw, the first to encounter Christian missionaries at the close of the eighth century, and were soon subjected to the Frankish realm which drew its spiritual guidance from Rome. Early in the ninth century, these influences expanded to Bohemia and Moravia, while the bold German political and missionary offensive which dispossessed the Slavs along the Elbe and the Baltic coast began at the same time and lasted nearly four hundred years.

During the second half of the ninth century, Byzantine Christianity penetrated Bulgaria, and political combinations in Moravia inspired the historic mission of Constantine and Methodius which, though fraught with far-reaching consequences for the Eastern Slavs, was barred from success in central Europe by the jealous opposition of the German clergy. The first quarter of the tenth century then witnessed an intense growth of Bulgarian culture under Byzantine influences which was destined to bear fruit after the conversion of Russia, and with the exception of the Croats, the Balkan Slavs all received the faith from Constantinople. Christianity was transmitted to Poland from Bohemia toward the middle of the tenth century. And finally, near the close of the tenth century, political events produced a situation in which conversion through Byzantine agency became advantageous for Prince Vladimir I of Kiev, through whose efforts the medieval Russians first abandoned paganism.

The Eastern Slavs, ancestors of the Russians, we found at the dawn of their history split up into sparsely settled and disunited tribal units, with a tendency to group themselves around trading posts and strong points strategically located on the course of the middle and upper Dnieper and on the northern rivers which empty into Lake Ladoga and the Baltic.

Conclusion 179

The first impulse to union was supplied in the ninth century by immigrant Swedish warrior-merchants exploring the Russian watercourse in search of a route to the Orient. As they settled in the primitive Russian towns along the Dnieper trade route, they established themselves as a ruling class, drew together the hitherto disunited Russian tribes and towns under the leadership of the Prince of Kiev, and were rapidly Russified by intermarriage with the native Slavs. Trade with Byzantium enriched the rulers of Kiev, and after 978 Vladimir transformed the previous loose confederation into a closely knit domain which extended from the Baltic to the Volga. From the time of his conversion the Russians rapidly absorbed the elements of Byzantine civilization, but from 1100 on the vitality of Kiev was sapped by princely feuds and the intensified menace of Asiatic nomads swarming across the southern prairies. A movement of migration to the safer northeast and the site of modern Moscow began at this period, and proved valuable for the maintenance of Russian national spirit and culture after the Tartars overran and subjected Russia in 1240.

The western principalities of Galicia and Lithuania which grew up after the decline and fall of Kiev eventually drifted into the Polish orbit, but with the gradual disintegration of the Tartar autocracy the fortunes of the princes of Moscow described a rising curve from the early fourteenth century. Successively defeating and absorbing domestic competitors, the Muscovites stood off the Tartars as their offensive power waned, and by the fall of Constantinople in 1453 Moscow became the residuary legatee of Eastern Orthodox tradition while it was tightening its control on the Volga and reaching out toward the Baltic coast. The struggle between the Muscovite throne and the feudal nobility was not finally settled until the reign of Ivan the Terrible, a contemporary of Queen Elizabeth, but during the previous century it became obvious that ultimate victory lay with the prince when Ivan's grandfather began to use the title of tsar.

The seventeenth century witnessed both the accession of the Romanovs and the institution of serfdom, though even before the time of Peter the Great the walls of Muscovite isolation were being battered as western techniques and cultural influences seeped in. This process was accelerated by the reforms of Peter and his successors in the course of the eighteenth century, during which Russia not only became recognized as a great European power but also began the process of catching up with Western culture and civilization which has continued to our own day. We have already traced the rise and fall of the early medieval Balkan principalities under Boris, Simeon, Samuel, and the Asen dynasty in Bulgaria between the ninth and the fourteenth centuries, and in Serbia under Stephen Nemanya in the twelfth and Stephen Dushan in the fourteenth century, but we noted that, except in the presence of an exceptionally able and energetic reigning prince, the centrifugal tendencies of the local nobility deprived both these states of a firm foundation. The resulting dispersion of effort prevented any effective resistance against the invading Turks, whose domination weighed heavily on the Balkan Slavs from the late fourteenth century well into modern times.

The conflict between German and Slav, a phase of which was fought out before our eyes during World War II, begun when Bavarian colonists began pushing the Slovenes back from the Danube during the ninth century, was inherent in the contemporaneous opposition of the Frankish and Bavarian priesthood to Constantine and Methodius, and was intensified by the process through which the Western Slavs were driven back from the Elbe to the Polish frontier of 1919. The colonization of the Baltic coastline by the militant German Order, which created the rivalry between Germans and Poles for the possession of the lower Vistula, and between Germans and Russians for the ownership or control of the southern shore of the Gulf of Finland, was an incident in the process of energetic German expansion which has kept this conflict alive.

The material and intellectual contributions of German

Conclusion

settlers in Bohemia and Poland, not only during the later Middle Ages but also in more recent times, were a vital factor in the progress of Western Slavic civilization. The very ideals of nationality which inspired modern agitation for the revival of Western Slavic national states sprang from the brains of German philosophers and political theorists. Even the basic concepts on which the dictatorship of the proletariat was erected in the Soviet Union stem from the theories of the son of a converted Jewish family in the Rhineland who was steeped in the philosophy of Hegel. After the kingdom of Bohemia became subject to the Hapsburgs in the sixteenth century, and after the partitions of Poland brought sections of the former kingdom under Austrian and Prussian sovereignty, the dominance of German influence in these areas was still more firmly established, and there can be no question that the Western Slavs, even under alien rule, participated fully in the advance of Western civilization with which they were in close and lasting contact.

Nationalist aspirations, as we have seen, developed during the first half of the nineteenth century and, while most keenly shared by the Western Slavs, were also transmitted to their South Slavic brethren by the Serbian and Bulgarian students who studied abroad. These aspirations were natural and logical. On the other hand, there was a marked tendency among the Western Slavs to minimize the economic security they enjoyed as members of larger states and to exaggerate the cogency of such traditions of national independence as they possessed. Their nationalistic sentiments were also stimulated both by the spectacle of the difficulties endured by their kindred under Russian rule and by the assumption of superiority by their German masters. There is no question but that the life of the Austro-Hungarian monarchy would have been prolonged had the constitution of 1867 been so modified as to grant its Slavic elements a degree of autonomy comparable to that possessed by German Austrians and by Magyars, since the Bohemians never secured equal political rights in Austria, while the Slovaks and the Croats were under an obstinately nationalistic Hungarian control. The Austrian opposition to legitimate Serbian economic aims also intensified Serbian agitation among the Southern Slavs within the monarchy, while the Austrian annexation of Bosnia and Herzegovina in 1908 was a direct challenge to Serbian national sentiment, and tended to make of Serbia a Russian pawn in the game of international politics—a situation the more dangerous because Bulgaria fell increasingly under the sway of German and Austrian diplomacy.

The interplay of foreign diplomatic influences in the Balkans was interrupted by the World War of 1914, and at its close interest naturally concentrated upon Central Europe where the French, with British support, were engaged in erecting a protective cordon of minor states around Germany. It is worth remarking that in 1914 Bohemian ambitions had not extended beyond vague hopes of eventual autonomy within a federalized monarchy, while the utopia of independence was conceived mainly in the minds of émigré leaders like Professor Masaryk and Dr. Beneš. It was not until 1917 that the domestic Bohemian attitude became definitely revolutionary, and Slovak sympathy was not finally secured until May, 1918, through the celebrated Treaty of Pittsburgh, which guaranteed the Slovaks a degree of autonomy which they never attained until just before the Czechoslovak Republic was dismembered by Hitler. As a matter of fact, the relations between Czechs and Slovaks were never so dovelike as Bohemian statesmen would have had us suppose, and at the Armistice, Czech troops had simply marched in and occupied the Slovak section of Hungary.

We now know enough of medieval Slavic history to realize why the process by which the Bohemian border areas were opened to medieval German settlement rendered dangerous in 1919 any boundary adjustment dictated by a spirit of revenge as a consequence of which these districts, for strategic reasons, were turned over to Czech rule. Eloquent warnings against this procedure were uttered at Paris by such eminent specialists in Central European affairs as the late Professor Archibald Cary Coolidge, but these warnings were fruitless because of the technical ignorance of the chief American delegates and of the strategical prejudices of the Allied Powers, whose statesmen were as poorly grounded in the essence of these problems as their American peers. In Poland as well, it is hardly necessary to recall that the establishment of the Danzig corridor was made risky by a series of complications which date back to the cession of certain Mazovian districts to the Teutonic Order in 1229, and were rendered still more serious by the various waves of German immigration which had created large German populations in every city of the district. Only a policy of determined self-restraint could have obviated friction between the ruling Poles and their new German subjects, and neither party had sufficient imagination or judgment to foresee the explosive consequences inherent in this situation.

The causes of World War II can thus be summed up in the fateful trio of revenge, strategy, and nationalism. If there is any lesson to be learned from the experience of the last thirty years, it is that setting up a series of economically weak national states solely on the basis of romantic ideals and strategic aims is no guarantee of peace. To bolster up their weak budgets or to favor local industry, such states erect tariff barriers which prevent the normal flow of commerce and exchange on which their very life depends. If their territories contain linguistic minorities, the latter are discriminated against in business and politics until they seek support from the nearest larger state to which they are akin, and eventually provide that state with a natural pretext for intervention. In order to counterbalance their more powerful neighbors or checkmate some adjacent state with good diplomatic connections, these little states unite in ententes and alliances which become the pawns of international politics, and give statesmen of these minor organisms a chance to assume positions of influence for which they are not qualified by experience or vision. But with the pro-